Go

This

Personality

Nathan Connell

Conza

Published in 2021 by Conza Books

ISBN Paperback: 978-1-8384791-0-7
Ebook: 978-1-8384791-1-4

A CIP catalogue copy of this book can be found in the British Library.

Published with the help of Indie Authors World
www.indieauthorsworld.com

IndieAuthors
World

Dedication

Nathan regularly said to his son, "I love my boy"....
AND HE DID. THERE IS NO DOUBT ABOUT THAT.

Introduction

NATHAN DAVID ARCHIE CONNELL, sadly passed away on the 27th of January 2020, aged 34. His dream was always to have the book on his life, that he had written, published. Although he never lived to see his dream fulfilled, it has.

How many of us reading this book have had one written or published? Not many I expect. This book has been published in honour of our son, husband, daddy, brother, nephew and friend.

This book has been written by Nathan, who suffered from mental health problems from a very early age. Attention Deficit Hyperactivity Disorder (ADHD) and Borderline Personality Disorder were at least two issues he had. There may have been others. For Nathan to have written this book over a period of 10 plus years and never to have lost sight of his dream to have it published is remarkable.

Nathan's book written by him, tells how he felt growing up. It also tells of his roller-coaster ride of a life. There was sadness, madness and badness. However, there was another side of Nathan that many others saw, but he either did not see, or did not want to mention in his book. I guess he would have seen it as, 'blowing his own trumpet'.

This additional read will tell of how Nathan on many occasions reached out to people in desperate need, those he saw lost and broken like himself. It will also tell you of the amusing things that he did and said, or some at least, as well as recorded comments others made about Nathan.

This is a tribute to Conza.

Shortly after Nathan's funeral in February 2020, a Church Minister sent me a photograph of an inscription carved on the wood in a courtroom in the Greenock Sheriff Court. It simply read, **'Conza'**.

Helping the lost and broken

A statement that sums up Nathan is, *'I'm not interested if you've stood with the great. I'm interested if you've sat with the broken'.*

Nathan once said that his siblings, Natalie, Benjamin and Bethany would never need God like he did because they were not broken. His sense of his own brokenness caused him to reach out to those who were also broken.

There was a man who moved into Kilmacolm who had a reputation as a Greenock hard man. Nathan met up with him and asked the man to come to his dad's meeting (a journey in faith support group). The man did and has been sober for a good number of years now. He sent a complimentary message about Nathan, after his death and said, "Hi David I would like to thank Nathan and you for everything you have done for me on my Christian walk. If I hadn't met Nathan I don't know where I would have been today".

There was a man in Bridge of Weir, who like Nathan, struggled with life controlling substances. Nathan did what Nathan did. He invited this man, named Colin, to come to his dad's group – 'The Bus Wi Nae Wheels'. This group was on each Thursday night. Before the group started each evening, there would be a time of prayer where the Church volunteers would do a huddle *(not a Celtic huddle I might add!)*. Colin sensed something of the reality of God that night and went on his own journey of faith. At the time of writing this book, he, Colin is a staff member at a Christian Centre. Colin's life changed by the Power of God without a doubt, but Nathan pointed him in the right direction. Colin has said, "Nathan planted the seed, telling me about the gospels and him getting excited about Jesus made me want what he had".

Christmas is a time for family, but sadly, many people have no family, or are alienated from them. Nathan knew a guy who fitted into the latter category. For the last three years, on Christmas day, Nathan had me take a Christmas dinner to this individual. I did not see anyone else reaching out to this poor unfortunate soul, BUT Nathan did. A simple act of kindness at Christmas.

Nathan also had Wilky join his family for Christmas one year because he was on his own. Wilky gets a few mentions later in the book, trust me!

Nathan a good number of years ago went with his mum and a guy he knew to buy him clothes. The guy needed new clothes, so Nathan bought him them with his own money. Fiona recalls that because the guy with Nathan was scruffy and he, Nathan was erratic-hyper in his behaviour, the security guard was paying close attention to them!

Around about 2010 – 2011, Nathan convinced his friend Dave to go to the Port Glasgow café on a Sunday evening. Each Sunday evening, people would share their personal stories of how through faith they had found freedom from addiction. At this meeting Nathan introduced Dave to Roy. Nathan kept asking Dave to go to the café and within a few weeks Dave went to rehab.

Nathan was so keen for Dave to go to rehab that he would ask him what he could do to get him to go to rehab. Nathan's question would be, "What can I do to get you to go away"?

Nathan and Dave grew up together and were always friends. Yes, they had their fallouts but remained close throughout Nathan's life. When they made amends to each other it was as if what had happened never had.

Dave says of Nathan, "He was bonkers at times". He remembers Nathan having a suitcase full of cigarettes when they were about 10. They didn't even smoke at that time!

Dave says, "Nathan liked people and had a heart. He was funny and wasn't stupid. He wrote a book".

The Court, the Cell, the Cop Shop

Nathan's lawyer told us a couple of stories from his interactions with Nathan in the courtroom and the cell (under the court where those in custody are held).

On one occasion, Nathan's lawyer had not yet arrived in court. Nathan was called before the sheriff and then sent back to the holding cell until his lawyer arrived. On arriving in court, the sheriff told the lawyer that his client was waiting for him to act in his defence, because in Nathan's words, the lawyer was "going to get the charges watered doon" (pronounced 'watird')! Probably not the best way to positively influence the sheriff.

Whenever Nathan was brought to court whilst being held in custody, his lawyer would always visit him in the holding cell. This time when he visited him, Nathan produced two playing cards that he had concealed in his boxers and gave one to his lawyer. Nathan's lawyer had worked with him since he was first in trouble with the law, from his teenage years. He knew how Nathan could be and that his behaviour was somewhat erratic at times. He waited for the message Nathan had to pass on using the two cards......They were both Jokers. Nathan said to his lawyer, "Remember to play the mental health card"! Simply meaning, lay it on thick to the sheriff about his mental health. Nathan's lawyer always did this, and it usually worked in his favour.

There was a time when Nathan was to appear at Paisley Sheriff Court and his lawyer could not be in attendance to speak on his behalf. His lawyer asked a colleague in the Paisley court to act for Nathan. Bad mistake. Bad judgement. The Paisley lawyer went to see Nathan and was told in no uncertain terms that, "a Paisley arse-hole" was not representing him! The Paisley lawyer told Fiona and I that if Nathan was a true representation of his lawyer's clients, he would not be defending any others.

Nathan had a warrant out for his arrest, and I drove him with a friend to Paisley police station so he could hand himself in. He would then be taken to court the following day. On approaching the charge-bar in reception, he announced to the police officer, "I was the gunman on the grassy knoll"! Nathan obviously thought this was funny, but the officer did not.

How those who knew Nathan described him

These are the words used to describe Nathan by some of those who knew him best, both friends and family members.

Character	Daddy
Caring	Loyal
Resilient	Legend
Protector	Courageous
Vibrant	Unique
Compassionate	Believer
Big-hearted	Uncle
Evangelist	Encouraging
Friendly	Unassuming
Sincere	Relentless
Respectful	Determined
Hilarious	Passionate

Robert surpassed himself when asked to give a word that described Nathan. His response was legend:

Loyal

Endearing

Generous

Empathetic

Noble

Dad

Other comments about Nathan were made and these are some of them.

"He was a great friend. He definetely inherited your trait of wanting to help the lost and broken" - Daniel

"You touched many people Nathan Connell and so glad you knew the Lord pal" - Frank

"So sorry to hear Nathan's passed. Ive not known him long but he was a kind soul" - Conor

"I am so heartbroken to learn of this. He was such a gentle soul with a beautiful spirit and heart" - Gaynor

"Truly gutted to hear this. Nathan was one of my childhood best friends" - Kenny

"Nathan was a great friend and always made me laugh" - Alex

"Nathan Connell, you were a gentleman" - Andrew

"Such a lovely young man and nephew" - Stephen

"Precious memories" - Jackie

"His life counted, he made a difference to so many" - David

"RIP Nathan ma man" - Brendan

"He was one of the good guys" - Rona

"Ye were a good man" - Finlay

"I liked Nathan a lot and always enjoyed it when he would visit" - Andrew

"Nathan may your massive heart live on" - Angela

"Beautiful person" - Fiona

"Legend. One in a million" - Rebekka

"He was and is and always will be amazing in his own unique way" - Shirley

"The journey continues. He will always have a place in my heart" - Ross

Benjamin, Nathan's brother has said, "Nathan was many things to many people. To me he was a brother. He would have done anything for me, or his family. Here is one story that encapsulates that. I had allegedly accrued a charge for a minor offence and was to be prosecuted. Nathan being Nathan told me to say it was him. Nathan hates, 'Grasses', but this was okay in his eyes. He was willing (wanting) to take the 'derry' for me. The only problem was that he was already incarcerated when the alleged offence took place! Brothers in arms. Love you and miss you always".

Natalie, Nathan's sister has said, "Forgiveness is the best form of love. Love you always, miss you always".

Bethany, Nathan's youngest sister has said, "I never thought this would be the chapter in my life that I would have to learn to be without my protector and you are no longer here to run to when life gets tough. Your words echo in my ear, "Chin up" and "What doesn't kill you makes you stronger" on a daily basis. I just wish you could hold me one last time. No words can explain the pain I feel every day since losing you. Sending you hugs, ice blasts and all the soggy chicken balls. Goodnight Nathan x".

Fiona, Nathan's mother and best friend has said, "My other children used to call Nathan my golden boy. Throughout all the chaos and madness I could never give up on him, or stop loving him because he had a heart bigger than himself. Loved to help people without boasting about it. He had a heart of pure gold".

Julie, Natalie's partner has commented, "We can't unwrite the past, and if we could this book wouldn't be half as interesting. Love you Nathan".

On Nathan's birthday, we his family, gathered and wrote words on balloons to him and then released them into the sky. Nathan's son, when asked for something to write on the balloon he was sending up to Heaven said, "I miss daddy. Love from Nathan and mummy".

Gemma, Nathan's wife has said, "Nathan, you left me beautiful memories, your love is still my guide and though we cannot see you Nathan, I'm sure you are by God's side".

Nathan's aunt Ailsa sent the words of a poem.

In Loving Memory of a special Nephew

The day you left and gained your wings my heart just broke in two

I wish you could have stayed with me but Heaven needed you

You left me with the memories and I love you dearly still

No matter how much time goes by you know I always will

You were a very special person with kindness in your heart
And the love we had together grows stronger now we're apart
I know I cannot bring you back although I wish it every day
But a piece of me went with you the day you went away.

Patman, one of Nathan's closest friends said, "One of a kind. Legend. Very, very, loyal friend".

Captain Pupek, another of Nathan's friends, who was like a brother to him said, "Nathan was loyal, big hearted, brave. He always went out his way to help others that needed help. Notorious and a true legend".

Wilky, a regular co-pilot with Nathan, in prison said, "The best way I can describe Nathan in one word was loyal. I've known Nathan since we were both 15. We both got into some mad situations over the years, but to give an example of the type of person/friend he was, I was in Barlinnie. I think it was 2008, possibly 2009. Nathan wanted to get off the drink. Instead of going to a group to deal with getting off it, Nathan decided to get a train up to Glasgow. Gets off at Central Station, buys a glass bottle of Irn Bru, walks until he sees a police car and smashes the glass bottle in front of the police car and gets lifted in Glasgow knowing he would go to Barlinnie. I am sitting in my cell and the peep hole opens. I think it is the screws doing their checks. It is Nathan, saying he had spoken to the screws and I was allowed to get dubbed up with him. So I packed my things and went and we became co-pilots. I asked him, "How did you know you would be in the same hall as mine, never mind the same cell"? He just laughed and said he knew because he prayed for it. Ha ha, he was some boy. Miss you bro".

Nathan's Eulogy by Callum

"I don't remember meeting Nathan; when I try he was just always there, in some of my earliest memories. Usually fretting that I would fall and hurt myself. He helped me name my dog. He taught me how to project spit properly. He protected me when I couldn't defend myself. In other words, he was like a brother to me. In fact, before I properly understood the term, I assumed that's what he was.

Nathan sometimes liked to remind me of a day while we were both still in primary, when I had wandered off from school and got lost and it was Nathan who found me and took me home safely. Maybe I was in no great danger that day; maybe someone else with good intentions would have found me. But the story mattered to us both because it was a reminder that ever since we were both just boys, before all the mistakes we both would make, Nathan was someone who would love and protect me for as long as he was able to.

So while many people can say with good reason that Nathan was no angel, growing up to me that's exactly what he was.

I've made a lot mistakes in life. I've hurt people. I've wronged people. Sometimes while they were trying to help me. Nathan never judged me. He just wanted to help, regardless of whether I had asked him to, regardless of whether he was in a position to give it.

I knew how hard life could be for Nathan. How he could be his own worst enemy. How in the last years of his life he fought his troubles for every minute of every day to stay sober.

So before he died, Nathan wasn't just a friend to me. He wasn't just a brother. He was an inspiration to me, in the way he lived his life to be a better man than the day before. How he strived to be a better father to his son. With how sincerely he wanted to help others avoid the mistakes which cost him so dearly.

That's how I'll remember Nathan, as an inspiration to us all".

When the 'wee man' heard his daddy had gone to Heaven, his response was one that would have made Conza smile and laugh. It simply was, "Hulk Smash".

So now it is time to read Nathan's story, in his own words and told in his own unique way.

David Connell (Nathan's dad)

Nathan's Introduction

My name is Nathan Connell and this is my story. My life has been one big ongoing roller-coaster and I have decided to write about it. I've read books and seen films *(based on true events)* and after finishing them I often thought that my life story would be more interesting.

You won't believe what I've been through and even though people will congregate and call me a liar, it has been incredible.

Personal note

Before you read any further, I would just like to apologise to everyone and anyone that I have upset through the years. And if this book offends, then you are trapped in hatred as I was. We've all done things we shouldn't have. Everyone has a past and adolescence is madness *(this book is about mine)*. This is not for the faint-hearted. Let's get started...

Chapter 1

I was born on the 25th of May 1985 in a small town in the West of Scotland called Greenock. My mother gave birth to me in the Rankin maternity ward in the Wren Road area. I was born on my granda's birthday.

My mum and dad are Christians, so I was named Nathan, a religious name that comes from the Bible. My name means **Gift from God.**

My older sister – Natalie was nearly two years older than me and we all lived in a small village near Greenock called Kilmacolm, which is on the outskirts of Port Glasgow.

The housing scheme we lived in was built to house the Americans who worked in the submarine base in Dunoon. The estate was nicknamed the 'Yankee' because of this.

Two years after I was born my mum had another son – Benjamin. We lived in Kilmacolm until I was four years old. I remember when I was three and I also remember my fourth birthday. I got a teenage mutant ninja turtle for my main present. I remember my mum and dad told me that they were all sold out and I couldn't get one but luckily, I got Raphael.

On my fourth birthday, I had a party and with my older sister we were playing outside when she fell on her knees over a broken glass bottle. She cut herself and had to go to the hospital for stitches. I remember carrying her home.

I also remember going to nursery school. And every Sunday I was forced to go to Church which I didn't always like. But at least I've always known that there is a God.

Chapter 2

Before I was due to start primary school, we moved house to Port Glasgow. We lived in a big house on Lilybank Road between Highholm Street and Gibshill (*which is in Greenock*). Our house was a stone throw away from Greenock which was the neighbouring town.

I then started school at Highholm Primary in the Port town. I hated my first day at school and every day after. In Primary 1, I used to put my fingers down my throat and make myself sick so that I wouldn't have to go to school.

My mum's great uncle was high up in the BB (*Boys' Brigade*) and me and my brother went to the one on Highholm Street, next to the Port Glasgow town train station. Then we moved to the Kilmacolm BB.

When I was very young, my dad let me watch some Bruce Lee films but my mum put a stop to it. My dad would sometimes secretly let me watch Universal Soldier and the Terminator. I always wanted to watch more fighting films, but my mum wouldn't let me.

To humour me instead, she took me to the video shop to choose a children's movie and I picked Problem Child. All the toys I wanted were swords and guns.

Even the children's films I was allowed to watch were swash-buckling adventures. I loved sword fighting and I hung around with an older boy. He was about eight and he had knives.

He gave me the holster of a combat knife with no blade. My mum had bought me children's cutlery and I took the butter knife and put it inside this empty holster. I hid a metal ladle and another blunt instrument so that I could play with my weapons.

I used to play in the grounds of the Lilybank Disabled School across the street from my house. There was a small enclosure with a gate on it used for putting wheelchairs after disabled children wet themselves. It was mostly empty so along with other children we used to play cops and robbers and we would use the drying cage as the dungeon. I was always a robber who escaped from the cage.

The house we lived in was 40 Lilybank Road and it was a big house with four floors. The basement was like another small house as well, with a living room, kitchen area, cellar, toilet and bedroom. There was also a back door which took you out to the garden.

One morning my mum and dad told me that the police came to my house in the middle of the night because of me. I was in bed sleeping. The officers never got my parents to wake me up they just told them to give me a warning, to stop phoning 999 and hanging up.

I told my mum and dad that it wasn't me, but they didn't believe me. After a while, my sister admitted that it was her who had done it (*but not to the police*). This was the first time the police came to my door because of me and it wasn't even me who done it! I was only six years old.

Chapter 3

My mum and dad liked the movie the Great Escape and I grew up watching the film. I used to go down to the basement and play in the cellar. There was a tunnel that went from the cellar along to where the kitchen space was. I used to imagine and fantasise that I was escaping from a POW camp and I would crawl through the tunnel with my butter knife tucked inside the holster.

I used to pretend that the police were soldiers and I would run away from them. I hadn't done anything wrong I just wanted them to chase me. I would climb onto the school wall and the police would chase after me. I loved doing this.

I later got banned from the Pakistani shop for stealing an ice pole. I was never allowed back in for shoplifting when I was seven.

My Mum moved me into Kilmacolm Primary School as our house in Port Glasgow was up for sale and we were moving back to Kilmacolm. I went to Kilmacolm Primary in Primary 2. A short time later we moved back to Kilmacolm, a house near the shops at the Cross. A year later, my mum and dad had another baby - Bethany.

We didn't know what sex the baby was. My mum didn't find out because she wanted it to be a surprise. But she got her Pastor to pray for a wee girl. My dad got me and my brother and sister to guess what date our baby sibling would be born. And I guessed right. It's like a part of me knew because my birthday (*and my granda's*) were both on the 25th and my cousin's was the 23rd May so I guessed that my mum's new baby would be born on the 24th of May. I was absolutely bang on. My wee sister was born the day before mine and my granda's birthday.

Not long after starting Kilmacolm primary I got sent home for the day for trying to kick my way through the cupboard door in the classroom because the teacher took my whoopee cushion off me and locked it away. That was the first time I got suspended from school, but it wasn't the last.

I didn't even realise why, but by the time I was in Primary 4, I wasn't allowed to play with any of the other children in my school or in Kilmacolm. I never got invited to any birthday parties or celebrations and I wasn't allowed in any of the other Kilmacolm kid's houses. I knew I would never be accepted again.

Whenever there was a party everyone else was invited except me. Children's parents would shout at me and give me abuse. I felt horrible and it's disgusting that a child was treated like this.

After the parties were over everyone in school would be talking about it and I was jealous. I felt empty but then I would find out that one or two other children didn't go either because they never got invited, so I would play with them. I would bond with all the other rejects but a short time later their parents would ban them from being in my company.

I first felt this rejection when I was a small child and by the time I was nine I was an outcast. Everyone thought that I was a wild child and this feeling of uselessness would stay with me always after that. It made me feel I couldn't do anything right. The only people who were there for me was my family.

The last time my mum was pregnant she wanted to have another baby girl. She prayed for this and her baby was a girl (*not a boy*) and out of happiness she called her Bethany-Joy.

Chapter 4

S chool was a nightmare. I was bursting with energy ripping through me and I had to sit every day on a chair for hours on end in a classroom. I know every child has to, but I couldn't handle it. I couldn't sit still or concentrate so with my happy hyperactive nature I became the class clown.

I remember being very proud because I was sure that I was the funniest person in the whole class. My head was racing so I would play up in class and cause trouble to pass the time. My whole Primary School life was getting into trouble. That's the Primary School memories I have, disruption and insubordination.

Every now and then I would break the last straw and be suspended from school or thrown out the class for a couple of days, having to work in the library with head teacher supervision.

The teachers would explain to the whole class telling us what to do but, because I couldn't pay any attention, I would shout out the answers (*if I knew them*) and the teachers would shout and scream at me all the time. This humiliated me in front of the whole class which made me feel horrible and all flustered. I would burst into temper tantrums and kick chairs over and throw things about the classroom and vandalise things.

I couldn't focus on schoolwork. I hadn't a clue what the teachers were saying because my head was in another place and I couldn't sit in silence and listen, to be able to concentrate or learn anything. I formed a self-mutiny within myself and rebelled against school because I could not listen.

I was rejected from everything, so I behaved badly for attention. I got myself into trouble to amuse myself and it was fun. Blowing raspberries in class was one of my favourite pastimes and still to this day makes me laugh.

The only time I behaved myself was when I was daydreaming. That's what I taught myself to do. Me behaving was me daydreaming.

I used to put drawing pins on the teacher's chair and I hated them all. When they were teaching the class, I would sit in silence imagining things that interested me, then the class would be instructed to start their work. I would look around and everyone else would be starting their class work except me. I was always the only person who didn't know what to do. This would freak me out and make me extremely agitated.

Even the simpletons knew what to do, while I sat in silence, kidding on that I was behaving and focusing but really my head was in another place.

My mum would cut out pictures of things that I wanted for Christmas and she sent me to school with it and told me to keep it in my desk. So that I could look at it and use it to make me behave. As my mum told me that if I got a bad report card, I would not get what I wanted for Christmas. Every year I got a bad report card, but my mum still bought me whatever I wanted.

My gran bought me a watch with a TV remote control on it. I wanted it so that I could switch off the television in school when the teacher put a programme on for the class to watch.

I used to panic when the class had to do tests, because I knew I wouldn't know the correct answers. I knew I wouldn't have a clue and I wouldn't be passing any tests. I used to lie to my mum and tell her I wasn't feeling well on the days of school tests, so I wouldn't have to go to school. I never ate breakfast, but I would eat some on the morning of tests, then I would put my fingers down my throat to make myself sick, in a desperate attempt to stop my mum sending me to school.

All the teachers picked on me and at the end of every year I always got a bad report card, so I felt I had nothing to look forward to or gain in school. I couldn't handle it. I was too hyper and couldn't (*wouldn't*) let them tell me what to do.

I would say that in school my behaviour was bad most days, if not every single day. Over the years I got suspended for different things. I stole pens out the teacher's desk, vandalised tables, stole books from the book club, then I set a dustbin on fire.

I lit a match and dropped it into the bin. It went up in flames and the janitor had to put the small fire out. I was then suspended because I tried to burn the bin in the playground to the ground.

Chapter 5

When things got too stressful at school, I would run home. This gave me a burst of energy and I would climb over the school fence and head back up the road through the Duchal Woods. When I ran away from school the head teacher would phone the police and the local police officer would come to my family home and take me back to school.

This was when I was first lifted by the police. I was nine years old.

I hated the teachers because they all picked on me and they told all the other children's parents that I was a bad influence. Everyone thought I was bad news and now the school got the police onto me, which made me hate the police as well.

This is where my hatred for the police first came from. I was lifted from my family home and taken back to school in the back of the police car. Back to my place of hate *(school)* and this made me hate the authorities.

A while later the local policeman died and I thought that meant that there would be no more policemen coming to take me back to school. I was right and wrong. From then it was always two uniformed police who came to get me. When the police took me back to school in the police car, I felt important.

Chapter 6

I refused to eat school dinners. At first my mum would make me a packed lunch and I would take it with me in my schoolbag, but then when I started running away from school I would just go home for lunch.

I would get a hot roll out of the bakers at the Cross, then I would go up the road with my lunch until school started back after lunch break. Then instead of going home with my lunch I would eat it then walk back to school with a couple of other boys.

Growing up I had everything I could ever want - the best of toys and clothes. I never wanted for anything. I have been on holiday to Malta, Corfu, Ibiza and France a few times.

My dad used to work for Prudential then for years he worked for the Royal Bank of Scotland and my mum was a nurse. My dad was working at a bank in Kilmarnock and he managed to get tickets to watch the Kilmarnock football team play. The first game was against Celtic which was the team I was brought up to support. At half time my dad went away to the snack bar to get me a 'Killie pie'.

For no reason I became scared that my dad wouldn't be able to find me, so I went looking for him and I ended up lost. I managed to make my way to the dugout where I saw an injured player lying on a stretcher on top of a table.

There was an announcement made over the tannoy and my dad came and got me. I then went back to Rugby Park to watch

Kilmarnock versus Rangers. This time we wanted Kilmarnock to beat Celtic's rivals Rangers, but Kilmarnock lost.

I was spoiled but the only thing I wasn't allowed was to watch violent movies and I was desperate to see them. The owner of the Kilmacolm video shop got me to dust shelves once a week for £4 and he would let me take a video tape home instead of paying me the few pounds cash and I always wanted violent movies.

The video shop man was an actor as well. He was an extra in the Scottish sitcom Rab C Nesbit.

I collected loads of violent films and I would watch them over and over. The first television that I got was a black and white one, which was also the first TV that my mum and dad had as well. Then I got a new coloured television (*& video combination*) in my bedroom and I would watch these violent adult films.

When a violent film came on the television I would record it in my bedroom and then watch it over and over, but that wasn't good enough I had to have the real video in the box so I would get the owner of the video shop to sell me a copy. When my dad found my video stash, he destroyed all of them and I felt sick. I felt as if I had lost a part of me and I was very anxious and agitated, but I would just dust more shelves and replace them again until I got my collection back.

One Friday night me and my brother went to my gran and granda's house to stay overnight, but we didn't sleep in their house. They let us spend the night in their caravan out in the garden. I loved the TV sitcom Father Ted so along with my brother we watched it that night in the caravan. The episode that came on was about Father Ted going to a caravan. It was a funny episode and a coincidence because we spent the night in a caravan too.

Chapter 7

In Primary 6 I got a male teacher and he was the best teacher I ever had. He never sent me to the head teacher's office once in the whole year, so I never got suspended and he even gave me a good report card. I never even got a single punishment exercise that whole year. That was the only year I got a good behaviour report card.

But then five days before the end of term I got suspended for picking up a butter knife in the dinner hall and holding it to someone's throat after I watched Braveheart.

My teacher was disappointed, so I apologised to him. He told me that I hadn't let him down I had only let myself down. I was then told to come back after the summer holidays.

I refused to go back to Kilmacolm Primary and I begged my mum to send me to another school for my last year. All summer holidays, I pleaded with her to put me into another primary for my last year before High School.

On my wishes my mum tried to put me into Bridge of Weir Primary but they wouldn't accept me, so I had to go back to Kilmacolm after the summer holidays for my last year.

One day my gran never turned up at work and my mum became worried, so she sent my older sister up to my grandparent's house to check to see if she was alright. But my sister Natalie found my poor gran dead in bed.

Natalie was 13 years old and she found my gran lying dead upstairs in her bedroom and for 20 years my sister would not go back up the stairs. My younger sister Bethany was only two years old, but she knew that the whole family was upset so she helped herself to a box of tissues and was handing them out to everyone who was crying.

My poor granda was left heart broken. Some years later he met a woman called Grace and he loved her too even though he always missed my gran. My gran was buried in the Kilmacolm cemetery and my granda would visit her grave with Grace and she would help clean the headstone which was a lovely thing for her to do.

At my gran's funeral the hymn, 'amazing grace' was sung and after my granda thinking that he couldn't go on another day after my gran dying, by God's grace he met Grace.

Chapter 8

After seven weeks summer holiday break (which didn't last long enough) I was back in the class for my last year at Kilmacolm primary. The head teacher walked into the classroom and I felt worried. I hated her and I wondered what she was doing in the class.

Suddenly I could feel a strange atmosphere. Something was going on. Sometime later, the bell rang and the whole school went out into the playground for a short break.

A famous football player had signed for Rangers and he put his wife's kids into Kilmacolm Primary. Everyone was all around his daughter and I felt a feeling of fame coming from her.

I got this footballer's autograph when he came to pick his children up from school. He parked his black Range Rover outside the school. I ran over to meet him for his signature. He had his hair bleached in white peroxide dreadlocks at this time and his car had tinted windows at the back.

He signed his full name on my jotter, and his nickname on the boy's jotter I was with. The janitor of the school was shouting at us to get away from this celebrity, but we just ignored him.

I played at football training one night a week after school. I was never picked to play for the school team because of my bad behaviour. I was never really any good, but I was fast.

You had to be in Primary 4 to go to football practice, but the celebrity footballer's son was in Primary 3 and was allowed to go. Other children's parents complained so he was stopped from going back to football practice. I remember playing football when the celebrity footballer's wife was sitting on the banking holding their baby.

From the 1990's I loved football. I watched the World Cup every four years and I watched football Italia every Saturday.

I've been brought up to support Celtic which is a Catholic team and when I was a child loved supporting Celtic, but then I got embarrassed that people would think that I was Catholic.

When the footballer, I mentioned joined Rangers he was superb and when his kids came to Kilmacolm Primary I tried to switch over to follow them, but I just couldn't do it. I wanted to be a Protestant so out of protest I gave up on football completely.

During the October holidays, we went to Poole in Dorset while my brother played in a pool competition. He won a holiday to play in the autumn tournament. While my family was watching, my wee brother got into the final and received a second prize and won £50. My brother was so small the staff at the caravan park were joking with him and asked him if he wanted a box to stand on because he could hardly reach the pool table. In the end, he nearly won the whole competition.

That previous summer I signed up for the first stage of the pool competition, but I went to the beach instead and my brother played on my behalf and won the free family holiday. My gran and granda went on holiday to Poole for years to Sandford Park where my brother played pool in Poole.

When we were away my dad told me that I wouldn't see the celebrity footballer's children again because he and their mother had split up, so I never saw his stepdaughter again. Years later I saw her on the television singing on the X-Factor.

When I was 10 years old, I tried smoking a cigarette with a boy I grew up with called Dave. It was horrible and very disgusting and I knew it was bad, but that is why I did it. I rebelled against my parents and I ran away from home and stayed out for the night. I hid in a wooden Wendy House in the grounds of my family's old Pastor. The garden I was hiding in was right across the road from the Kilmacolm police station. I could hear the police car going in and out of the police station while they were looking for me. I was hiding right under their noses. While I was hiding in my old Pastor's garden, it might seem odd, but I felt close to God.

Chapter 9

O ne day I was sitting in school when the teacher left the class. With a boy, we both made our way into the wet area of the classroom without permission or supervision. We started to play-fight when I accidently hurt the boy. He let out a hurtful moan and I knew that I'd hurt him. I didn't mean it, but the next day the boy never came into school. Later that day, I was taken back into the classroom where the wet area was, by the head teacher.

There were two classrooms joined onto each other with the wet area in the middle which both the classrooms shared. The other classroom was empty and there were two women sitting at a desk.

The head teacher told me that the women were the police, but they never looked like normal officers, they were dressed in office suits. They were the plain clothes police (*CID*).

The 'cops in disguise' asked me what happened the day before in the wet area as they pointed it out to me. I felt some sort of loyalty to the boy I had hurt and I knew that it was an accident, so I told the police the truth. They then told me that I had concussed the boy and he was taken to the hospital with a head injury.

I felt really bad and guilty even though I didn't mean it. When the boy who I accidently assaulted came back to school, he told me that his dad was an officer who worked in the jail. This spooked me out and the boy's sister always gave me a mean look every time I saw her.

When it came time for me to go to High School my mum and dad tried to put me into Gryffe High in Houston, but I got a knock-back. My parents appealed the decision and after a legal battle I was accepted. They had to let me in because my older sister was in that school so because my sibling was there, I was to go also. This was something the teachers would regret.

Because I never got into Gryffe High at first, I had to go to Port Glasgow High school for the induction day and I was meant to go back after the summer holidays. I didn't want to go to the Port High because I broke the head teacher's hand by accident.

The head teacher was doing volunteer work at the Saint Columba's Church Youth Club across the street from my house and I was playing up, so he tried to restrain me. I wriggled and wriggled until I broke free and I ran out and then I was banned for life. I was told that I had broken the High School teacher's hand.

I never had to attend Port Glasgow High school after that induction day. A week before the first term was due to start, I got accepted into Gryffe High school.

I was glad I didn't have to go back to the Port High where the teachers would no doubt pick on me for breaking the head teacher's hand. I didn't have to go back to Port Glasgow High school which was 'handy'.

Chapter 10

High School was a fresh start for me where none of the teachers knew me and it went okay for a couple of weeks, but then frustration lead to disruption in the class. I was then put on a behaviour card.

Also, for my bad behaviour I was also put on detention for weeks. The teachers didn't want me out and about around the school ground. They could keep an eye on me in the classroom, but they never knew what I could be doing outside. I wasn't trusted so I was controlled in the school or put out the school.

When I was suspended, I would come back to the school at lunchtime with other boys and some of the head teachers would chase us away. They were wearing suits and chasing after me with their walkie talkies.

I started to get into trouble away from school with the police for smashing windows. I would take empty bottles from the glass bottle bank in the car park in Kilmacolm and smash them through the windows of the Community Centre.

There were two Community Centres in Kilmacolm, one right at the Cross and another one over in the car park. I liked the wee man who ran the one at the Cross, so I didn't smash his windows just the Community Centre at the car park along with cars that were parked there.

The first time I got suspended (from Gryffe High) was for ripping my behaviour card up. I was excluded for three days. That night I went down to the Yankee Land in Kilmacolm where my music teacher lived and I threatened to smash her windows as I ran through her garden shouting abuse at her. She shouted back at me and told me she was getting the police.

We were learning how to play the recorder but I'm not musically gifted, so I sat in silence. I didn't make a sound and I wouldn't say that I was misbehaving at all, but the music teacher wrote on my conduct card that my behaviour was unacceptable. I wondered why and I said to her that I didn't do anything, but the teacher said exactly (*you didn't do anything*). So, my behaviour was scored unacceptable. This was a behaviour card or so it seems. It was not a pupil's hopes of musical dreams.

Chapter 11

Not only was my behaviour in school terrible, but I had been arrested many times for smashing windows and cars. I ended up getting a social worker and then had to attend the Children's Panel.

The first hearing that I went to was because I had been charged with smashing over 100 windows. I smashed 50 then when they were fixed, I smashed them again. I got arrested for breaking into the Youth Club and stealing all the sweets and chocolates.

I also got charged with perverting the course of justice for giving a false name to the police. I got away with it once or twice but then the police made it their business to know me.

When I got charged with telling lies to the police, they would even slap me about when I was only 12 years old. They used to intimidate me and scare me when I was a wee boy. They treated me like scum and when I lied to them, they would try and terrify me. It worked; they really did frighten me and this made me hate them even more.

Getting into trouble and being bad became my identity. That's how everyone knew me and by this point I got the blame for everything, whether it was me or not and causing havoc was now my status.

For years there's been a Cattle Show in Kilmacolm every summer. Along with another two boys we all went to the Kilmacolm and Port Glasgow Agricultural Show. Between me and Dave we decided to steal a woolen fleece from a clothes rack. We didn't get far when the police caught us. The officer who single handedly arrested us never took us home or to the police station. He gave us a warning and let us go. We were both lifted by the police for trying to fleece a fleece.

Chapter 12

In school, the only subjects I was ever interested in were English and Technical. At first, I liked French but then because of my behaviour the head of the department picked on me, so I went off learning this foreign language.

One English lesson the teacher took our class to the library and we were all told to pick a book to sit and read. I found a big hard back book called movie media and I sat down and flicked through this big, interesting book. I looked through the pages and, in my search, I found a chapter on *'banned movies'*. I stopped and read about all these unsuitable violent films. It listed the movies that were banned and there were paragraphs on the films which told you the story lines.

I read about a British movie that was deemed so horrific the films own director banned it in 1971. Stanley Kubrick pulled the plug on his own masterpiece **A Clockwork Orange** and shut the show down (*for as long as he was alive*).

When I read about this, I felt something inside me drawing me towards this film. I was in first year at High School. It was 1997 and the film had been banned for 24 years (*the longest film that had ever been banned*) and now I was desperate to see this evil film.

That night after school I went into the Kilmacolm video shop and asked the owner if he could get me a copy, but he told me no one could get it in this part of Europe. Over the director's dead body would the film be shown again.

There was a boy in my class and his dad had a video shop too and I asked him to try and get it for me. I was at my wits end trying to get my hands on a copy of this unsuitable film, but I failed and I couldn't get it anywhere.

One Saturday me and Dave went on the bus to Greenock. I don't know whose idea it was but between us we both decided to get one of our ears pierced. After we got it done, we couldn't stop laughing, but when I got home my mum made me take it out. She pulled the stud out of my ear.

Dave's parents let him keep his earring in. I was gutted that I wasn't allowed to keep mine, but then after a while my dad let me get my ear pierced again. Shortly after this I got my other ear pierced too. I wore gold hoops in both ears.

My dad told me never to get Indian Ink - tattoo. At that time, I didn't even know what that was, but then when I was 15, I bought a bottle of it and started giving myself and Dave home tattoos. I still have some tattoos to this day. The others I got covered up and lasered away.

Chapter 13

After a few months of waiting I ended up getting put into a hospital day care to be assessed. I started going to Larkfield Child and Family Centre in Greenock every Tuesday. I was gutted when I first had to go but a boy I knew from Kilmacolm called Adam was in there too, so we had a lot of laughs. We were assessed there every Tuesday for six months.

I was diagnosed with ADHD. I was certified as an extreme case. And the psychiatrist said that my ADHD was so bad that I couldn't handle school full time, so I was taken out at 12 o'clock and sent to day care in the afternoons.

The doctor at the Larkfield Unit put me on medication. I started on Ritalin then went onto Imipramine. It was this doctor who decided what happened to me now that I suffered ADHD.

I was put into day care in the afternoons called the Mearns Centre in Greenock. I quite liked it. I went there three days a week.

When most children get diagnosed with ADHD, they are normally in primary school. I was a teenager at High School when I got certified. My mum and dad went to an ADHD support group where other children's parents went because their children also had this condition. I was the oldest out of everyone.

As soon as Gryffe High School found out I had ADHD, I was discriminated against. I always got suspended, frequently for three days at a time for chaotic classroom behaviour, but now I got suspended for weeks on end, because I was certified as a child with behaviour problems. My family thought that I was mad but everyone else thought that I was bad.

Chapter 14

I got in with the crowd and I was introduced to hash. A short time later I tried alcohol. I was 12 years old and I was putting myself into the drink and drugs scene. I only went with the flow; these were not my own ideas.

I couldn't handle school and my behaviour was terrible so why wouldn't I try drink and drugs? I just wanted to be normal and at that time normality was trying these substances.

I knew it was bad, but I smoked a joint with a boy anyway and we hit the giggles and couldn't stop laughing. It was exciting. This was the first time in my life I had ever been under the influence of anything. I was 12 years old and I began smoking as much hash as I could.

The neighbours in our old close all shared our garden, so they used to all club together and pay a communal bill for gardeners to cut the grass out our backdoor.

The gardeners were two brothers (*in their 20s*) and a 16-year-old boy. When they were out my back garden cutting our grass, I took them cups of tea and chocolate biscuits, so they let me smoke their hash with them.

But the gardeners took more than hash, they were on other harder drugs and they would all fight each other. The older brother stabbed his younger brother in the face with a broken glass bottle. Then the young man repaid his older brother by knocking him to the ground on my street, with a single punch bursting his eye.

A year later the teenage gardener ended up in hospital with his face smashed in. The younger brother smacked him on the chin and broke his jaw.

Doctors gave the boy strong painkillers and he was sent home. He then overdosed and died in a flat in Bridge of Weir. The boy lived next to my granda and his dad told me that it wasn't illegal drugs that killed his son. He put a notice in the Greenock Telegraph stating that post-mortem results were an overdose on prescribed medication.

Things didn't go much better for the two brother gardeners. The youngest killed a man and the oldest killed himself. That was the life of three Kilmacolm gardeners until they all lost it, except the brother who was jailed for life. Only he has his life left but also a life sentence to serve.

After I tried hash at 12, I began smoking as much cannabis as I could and by the time I was 13 hash and green were seen to be my teen scene.

Chapter 15

Not long after I tried smoking hash, along with some other boys I tried alcohol. I drank a litre of White Lightening Cider and it tasted horrible. The other boys were drunk, but I couldn't walk and was sick everywhere. I felt ill. I was lying on the ground spewing all down myself. I was spinning and it was awful. I hated it. I didn't want to drink ever again. I did not like alcohol, but I smoked cigarettes every day and I always wanted more hash.

Then one night with another boy, we chipped in and bought a bottle of Buckfast Tonic Wine in Bridge of Weir. At first, I didn't want to drink again because of what happened to me on the cider, but I was told that Buckfast was a good drink and now I knew that cider was not. So, I shared a bottle with another boy.

The both of us each took drink for drink until this bottle of wine was finished and we were both drunk. The feeling I had was more like a buzz and I did like it. Then soon after this I drank a full bottle by myself. I was with two other boys and we all got one each and I felt really good and I honestly liked it a lot.

Soon after I tried wine, I started getting a bottle on Friday and Saturday nights. Very quickly I lived for the weekend where I drank both nights. I used to wait at the shops until I met an adult who would go in and get a bottle for me. Here I was 13 years old and I had fallen in love with Buckfast. I stopped going to Church I refused to go. I just done my own thing *(which was drink and drugs)*.

I met a boy in Bridge of Weir called Paul and I would drink and smoke hash with him, but once he was under the influence of alcohol, he became aggressive and this frightened me. If I was drunk, I wasn't scared, but if I was in his company when I was sober, I felt like an oddball. I didn't like Paul at all when he drank alcohol.

35

Chapter 16

One day I got suspended for 20 days for a petty incident. I stole a packet of jotters out the teacher's cupboard. Of course, I didn't even need them I was just a rascal.

My social worker came to my house and my mum was standing on the stairs in my close talking to him. I went down behind them and closed the storm-door and locked it.

I went into the kitchen and I took all my medication from the cupboard. Then I took a big drink of Fanta and I swallowed all my medicine; I didn't want to live anymore.

I was only 13 and now I knew that I had something wrong with me. I was drinking and smoking cannabis regularly because this was what my generation done. I just wanted to be normal, but I couldn't handle school which made me feel I wanted to end it all. I didn't want to live my life anymore. I was only 13, but I felt I could not go on another day.

My mum was banging the door, but I wouldn't open it until I felt really dizzy and hot and sweaty then I freaked out. I knew I was going to die. So, I opened the door and let my mum and my social worker back in. They saw the state of me and they realised I had taken an overdose.

My mum phoned an ambulance and I was taken to hospital. The nurses made me drink this charcoal stuff to make me sick. After I spewed it all back up, I passed out. I woke up in hospital a day later.

When I went back to school after the 20 days suspension, all the teachers were picking on me even more and I just couldn't handle that school anymore. The assistant head teacher was the head of the geography department. I didn't like geography and I didn't like him. I threatened him and I told the head of the whole school to, "Fuck Off".

I went back to another panel and because I had been diagnosed with ADHD and had tried to kill myself, I had to go to a residential school miles from home. There was nothing I could say I was sent away.

Chapter 17

I t was January 1999; I was 13 years old and I was sent to an all boy's residential school in Dundee. Not to be reformed but educated. I was prescribed different medications and I was told that I would have no problem passing my exams. Because I wasn't stupid this was the place for me. I would be able to sit my Standard Grades and was a chance for me to do well educationally.

At this time there were only two schools in Scotland that boys like me could get a decent education and Parkview was one of them, but I was told I would be in there until I was 16 so this broke me.

No one I knew at that age was depressed as a teenager - life is good but not for me. I was put to this place of misery.

This is when I learned that if you don't behave yourself you will get sent away, but I couldn't behave I was just so frustrated. I was 13 years old and mischievous and because of this I was sent to live in a boarding school for young boys with behaviour problems.

I was only a child. I was in my first year as a teenager and I was put in this place until I was a legal age to leave at 16. I was supposed to accept it and make the most of over two years in Dundee.

The government paid over £900 a week for my placement, but I was hardly ever in the building. I hated being away from home, so I ran away every chance I got. I used to head to the Dundee train station and skip the train to Glasgow, then get the bus to Kilmacolm, as the driver let me on for free.

I had shoplifted before and in case I never made it back home to Kilmacolm, I headed to a shop on Perth Road and stole a bottle of Buckfast off one of the shelves. Then I went and drank it by myself and made my way drunk to the train station. I never cared if I made it. At least I was drunk. I did make it back home at different times, but I got caught loads as well.

At different times I ran away with most of the other boys in the school, but if I had no-one else to run away with, I ran away on my own.

I already had a taste for Buckfast before I was sent away but now, I turned to alcohol to solve my problems. I was only 13 years old and I would get drunk by myself.

I didn't make it back home all the time. I got caught by the police a lot and I was locked up in the cells in the police stations in Dundee, Perth, Stirling, Glasgow, Johnstone, Paisley and Greenock and for the first time in my life I felt notorious. The movie the Great Escape inspired me. When I was locked up in the cells, I thought I was being held in the cooler. I used to take my socks off and stuff them with toilet roll, making a wee ball and I would throw it about the cell. Because I was drunk, I didn't care at all. At least I had my ball.

Chapter 18

I n the end up I couldn't get drink from the local shop. They put a sign up on the window saying 'no children allowed during school hours' and brought in security guards. So, we robbed other off sales.

My head was racing at 100 miles an hour constantly, all day, every day, so whenever I was locked up in the police station for the few hours, it was the only thing that calmed me down, not any medication. I never took my medicine. I have been prescribed different meds since I was 13, ever since I got diagnosed with ADHD, but I didn't take them, I ran away.

Parkview gave you six cigarettes a day, but I was hardly ever in the building, so I didn't get any. You had to earn your pocket money and if you smoked you could buy your cigarettes so the boys who didn't smoke had more money, which is the same in all walks of life.

I never got any pocket money because I never earned any. I always ran away and I would smash the place up. Even when I ran away, I would break a glass tube on the fire exit and run down the fire escape. So, I would get billed for that too.

I got restrained a few times in the school in Dundee. Once for trying to run away my collar bone was dislocated because the head teacher caught me and rag dolled me. After that I knew that when I was going to run away, to do a disappearing act and vanish.

When I came back, if I didn't run away for a few days, they still wouldn't give me any cigarettes until I earned them. Due to this I refused to take my medication unless I got to smoke, but the head teacher would only give me one cigarette at nighttime which he called a dog's chance. I had to take my medication though and obviously not run away. I did comply occasionally but one cigarette wasn't enough for me so I would run away and one way or another I would find a smoke. I found a factory with a smoke room and I would run in and steal packets of cigarettes while the workers were working.

On my 14th birthday my family drove through to Dundee to take me out for a meal and to give me presents, but I had forgotten it was even my birthday. The school gave me a Wranglers watch which I still have to this day, but it has never been worn. It was my birthday and I had forgotten. Which was an utter shame.

Another time my aunt and uncle drove through from Aberdeenshire to take me out for something to eat, but I had already run away so when they got to the school, I never got to see them.

Some people from Dundee call people from Glasgow 'Weegies'. Port Glasgow is 20 miles from Glasgow. One time I ran away from the school - Parkview and a girl attacked me and she was screaming, "Weegie" at me. I told her that I wasn't from Glasgow, so she stopped punching me and said, *"sorry pal, where are you from?"* When I told her (*Port Glasgow*) she started hitting me again.

I was away from home at a young age and I decided to keep running as long as I could. I wouldn't be able to run away from secure and I was constantly told that's where I was going, but I didn't care. I knew I was already on my way there.

Chapter 19

I ran away with three boys, but we didn't make it far when the Dundee police caught us. We were all taken back to Parkview, but weren't put back into our own rooms, we were put in a different bedroom for the night.

In the middle of the night, two of the boys started masturbating each other. I freaked out and I was terrified. I've been sexually active since I was 12 and I kissed girls, but this put a fear right through me. I told the staff what had happened although I did feel like a rat for telling tales, but I refused to talk to the police and the two boys denied it.

One of them went home to Edinburgh and refused to come back to Parkview so he was sent to another residential school in that city. The other boy ended up getting sent to Saint Mary's secure unit for children, because within a week he 'beasted' another boy who was thought to be crying wolf.

After this happened, I was going to run away again but then the staff told me that we were all going to a swimming competition. I was a good swimmer, so I decided not to abscond that day and I went to the swimming pool with the school. I won basically every race at all the different strokes and I was given a few swimming certificates. This was the first time in my life that I had ever achieved anything. I felt proud of myself. The staff told me I had potential and should stop absconding. But there was nothing they could say, the next day I became a stray and ran away.

Chapter 20

I got moved rooms twice while I was in Dundee and most of the bedrooms had two or three beds in them. I would corrupt any fellow roommate to abscond and could have convinced a boy in a wheelchair to run away with me.

I even worked my way round all the boys asking them individually to run away with me. I made a decision to fight the system. Since I was 13 years old, I was at war with the system within my heart. I was away until I was 16 and made the decision to run away as long as I could.

Sometimes I would be on the run for up to a week. When I made it back to Kilmacolm I went over to my girlfriend's house in Bridge of Weir and she would feed and hide me. I could not go to my family home because the police would arrest me on the spot.

Police officers came to my girlfriend's house looking for me and I would hide under her bed and she would even lie to the police telling them that she did not know where I was. Her mum didn't even know that I was hiding in her house for days at a time.

In the school in Dundee, the head teacher took all my clothes off me and I was forced to wear my pyjamas. This was to prevent me from running away but it did not work I still ran. I went to the Dundee train station wearing my pyjamas and slippers. I got on the train and I hid in the train's toilet for over an hour and I made it to Glasgow Queen Street. Then I walked to Buchanan Street Bus Station where I got the bus to Bridge of Weir.

The staff at the school told me I would never make it back home dressed in my pyjamas because the police were watching for me and I had no chance.

But I travelled 80 miles on the train and a bus with no money wearing my pyjamas, dressing gown and slippers. I stuck out like a sore thumb, but I went for it again and made it. That night I turned up at my girlfriend's house where I hid. I was ready for bed anyway.

Chapter 21

I was on the run from the school and I was hiding out at my girlfriend's house in Bridge of Weir. She was at school and I went out for a walk.

As I walked around the corner I passed by a professional footballer's house. His car was parked outside (*a black BMW convertible*). I climbed in and sat on the driver's seat and suddenly I could feel that I was sitting on something hard and uncomfortable. I lifted myself up and put my hand under me and grabbed what I was sitting on. It was the car keys.

I got a rush of excitement. I started the car and tried to drive it. I didn't know how so I just stalled and smashed my face off the steering wheel.

I took the keys, got out the car and ran. I also found a letter in the glove compartment written to the car owner. I took that too. It wasn't just the car keys; it was his house keys as well.

I hid the bulky set of keys in the cupboard at the bottom of my close in Kilmacolm. I got captured and taken back to the school in Dundee. I told the other boys that I had car keys for a famous footballer, but they didn't believe me. We went out to try and steal other cars anyway.

Later I went back to the footballer's house to try and take his cracking car again, but it was gone. He must have moved it using his other set of car keys.

I knew I also had his house keys, but I wouldn't break into someone's house and storm the place. I stashed the keys in my room with the letter I had taken from his car too. I hid them in the cupboard in my bedroom until my dad found them. My dad is a Celtic fan but a born-again Christian, so doing the decent thing he made sure the footballer got his keys back.

The Dundee school was a big castle type building next to Dundee's Balgay Park. On the grounds of the school there was another building which was the residential campus for students at Dundee University. The university was along the street from the school and the student's campus was on our grounds. We were to stay away from them, but we shared the football ground together which we used separately.

I didn't know it back then, but the big hit computer game *Grand Theft Auto* was made by students at Dundee University. I can't help but wonder if maybe they might have lived in the campus on the grounds of the school, where I was supposed to live for over two years. The first *Grand Theft Auto* game was made in 1997 and I was sent to Dundee in 1999. The students who made the Play Station phenomenon are now Rock Star Games.

The children's panel sent me to Dundee to be educated in the city where the computerised creation came from. I was running all over a part of Scotland wearing only my pyjamas and trying to steal cars in the process. I lived and experienced my own personal *Grand Theft Auto*.

Chapter 22

I ran away with another boy and we ended up drunk at the Dundee train station. We were waiting on the train to Glasgow where we met a man who was also waiting on the train. This man was going to London but had to stop at Glasgow first. We got talking to him and he offered us the keys to his flat in Dundee. Acting on impulse and being drunk I quickly took the house keys in hand and we left the train station.

Another man we met drove us to Rosefield Street, where I stayed in the flat for about a week. When I was hungry, I walked into a shop and stole pot noodles and crisps.

For no reason other than boredom I smashed up the flat with a wooden rolling pin. Someone must have heard the smashing noises and phoned the police and they came flying through the door. I was arrested and taken to Dundee's Bell Street police station.

One of the police officers told me that the man's house that I was staying in was a paedophile. I didn't believe the policeman at the time. I thought he was trying to scare me but maybe he was right which is terrifying. What if the man came back to his flat while I was still inside?

A few hours later the police took me out of my cell and I was taken back to school where I was told that I was expelled. I was then put back in another police car. They never told me where I was going, so I automatically thought that I was going to secure. I was meant to be on my way to Saint Phillips approved school in Airdrie, only it never happened.

Whilst I was being driven on the motorway from Dundee, a message came through on the police radio that Saint Phillips were refusing to take me. The 'delivery driver' turned the car around and I was driven back to Dundee and I was taken back to school. This time I could not run away.

I was put in my room with members of staff sitting with me and there were more outside my room. I was expelled but I would not be able to run away. The school was keeping me until an emergency panel meeting on the following Monday.

It was Tuesday and I wasn't left alone for a single minute. They had to bring in staff to do overtime. This was the only time where I knew I couldn't abscond.

On the Thursday I was told that I would be going home the next day for the weekend until my panel on Monday. I was very happy at this. I was sincerely hoping from the bottom of my heart, that the panel would let me be and not put me somewhere else.

Maybe I was going to get put into a secure unit, but I didn't care. Obviously, I would have rather stayed at home but at least my days in Dundee were over.

When the head teacher told me that I was expelled I didn't care. The next day the Dundee police came and charged me with about 20 shopliftings (*Buckfast*). I was also charged with breaking into cars to steal money and cigarettes.

I would talk other boys into running away with me, then when they did, I would organise things so that we steal alcohol from the shops. Some of the other boys would help themselves to beer and cider but I only stole wine every time. Some of these boys had never tried tonic wine beforehand and I gave them their first drink of it. I thought I was doing them a favour by letting them savour my introduction to the Buckfast flavour.

Chapter 23

I wanted to stay at the family home, but the panel wouldn't let me. Monday came and I went to another children's hearing, but I wasn't locked up in secure. I was put into Newfield Resource Centre in Johnstone under a three-week warrant.

This children's home was where kids were held so that the staff could assess the child's background. The carers then came to a decision whether the child was fit to go home or had to go somewhere else.

I was putting my own life in danger absconding from residential school and running all over different parts of Scotland. I picked up more charges that I had before I was sent away. I was 14 years old and now I was a juvenile delinquent.

I was only put in a children's home because residential school didn't work but the panel wouldn't let me go home. I was told I was out of control. I had been fighting the system ever since I was sent into residential school, six months before. I wasn't locked up because I was never violent. I was educationally out of control.

The children's panel weren't letting me go back home to live with my family. I was told that it wasn't suitable to be with my family. I had to be cared for by residential staff in a unit for children who needed to be looked after.

Since I went to the Dundee school, at every panel there was talk of me getting locked up in a secure unit, but it never happened. There were no spaces and I wasn't that bad anyway.

The plan was now for me to work my way back home. I handled the Johnstone Centre better than Dundee because I was only six miles away from my family home. All I wanted was to go home and the Johnstone Centre told me they would get me there. Like all good assurances from the system there was a catch. I had to take my medication (*I was prescribed a new batch*).

Chapter 24

My psychiatrist ordered me to start on fluoxetine (*Prozac*) and there's no other way of explaining this than the way it happened. The staff dangled my medication in front of me and said, "*take these and you will go home*". I jumped at the chance and took these capsules.

I was given my happy pills at night time, which led to me having a rush of excitement, but I couldn't sleep, so they changed my medication time to the morning while the staff were waiting for my happy hour.

Prozac changed my sense of humour for the rest of my life. I was smoking hash in the Johnstone Centre, which made me laugh even more.

I didn't run away from the Centre. I kept my head down and spent my pocket money on hash. I would get stoned there as much as I could and I stopped drinking for a while.

As soon as I got sent to Dundee, I was put in a hole and all I wanted was to get out of it. I didn't have a care in the world about my education I just wanted to go home. I know I dug the hole even deeper for myself, but I had lost everything. I had everything at home, but I was sent away.

Now I lost my only hope of a proper education tutored to me by professionals for my needs. All I wanted was to go home and I was told that I could be home in a few months and not another two years.

When I went to residential school my education was finished. I never got to pick my subjects and I never sat any exams or prelims.

The panel put me into the Johnstone Centre under a supervision warrant. If I ran away from there, the police had a warrant to arrest me and take me back to the panel where I was told I would be locked up in secure. I changed my mind about being locked up. I just wanted to go home.

Obviously, I had to stop breaking the law and offending. I never ran away once in the three-week warrant. So, when I went back to the panel, the warrant was lifted. I had a Safe Guarder (*children's lawyer*) appearing at the panel and writing a report.

About a month later I was given a home leave for a few hours. A short time later I was given an overnight home leave. And within a few weeks I started getting home leaves at the weekends. I started to like the Johnstone Centre. I didn't want to run away. I always had a home leave to look forward to.

One time I was on a home leave and a staff member came to pick me up to take me back to Johnstone but he crashed the car and nearly died and I never got picked up that night and I stayed at home.

I worked my home leaves up to six nights a week, meaning that I was only in the Centre one night a week but then one day whilst on a home leave, I came up with a brainwave.

I decided to buy an air gun. With another boy who I met in the Centre we both went to a shop in Paisley looking at air guns. We were both too young to get served but we met a man and I gave him the money to go in and buy me a 2.2 slug gun.

We got the bus back to Kilmacolm where we met another guy, who told me that he had a 1.77 BB gun which he would sell me for a tenner. So, I arranged to meet the guy and I bought this other BB gun from him. Now I had two air guns. I gave the boy I was with the 2.2 one while I kept the 1.77. The 2.2 was the most powerful but it only fired one pellet at a time whereas the 1.77 loaded over 10 pellets or ball bearings and it looked like a real gun.

We were walking about Kilmacolm with an air gun each. And then I shot the 1.77 at a window of a boy who used to bully me. He came running out and grabbed the 2.2 off the boy I was with.

I ran away with the 1.77 and planked it somewhere safe. We only had the 2.2 for a few hours then it was taken from us by a witness who handed it over to the police. Police came and we were both charged. The other boy blamed me for the whole thing and he told the police that I had the BB gun, but they never got it. I kept it hidden away. All my home leaves were then stopped.

After being in the Johnstone Centre for six months the building was getting renewed, so we all moved to Gryffe Home in Bridge of Weir. This made me even happier because I was only three miles from home.

Newfield had a school and so did Parkview (*school*) but the Gryffe Home didn't have an education department, so the boys were sent to Kibble and the girls were sent to Good Shepherd. I still had to live in Gryffe/Newfield, but I started going to Kibble as a day boy.

Kibble was an approved school in Paisley across from the Glasgow airport. When I first walked in, I heard the noise, coming from all the bad boys.

Chapter 25

I got punched twice in Parkview but in the Kibble, I got battered. Two boys smashed me about the play station room in the day unit. It was a practical joke that went wrong.

In the technical woodwork class, a boy bent down to pick up a piece of wood and I stuck a six-inch nail in his backside. I didn't stab him I was only joking. I was 14 and I thought it was funny, but this boy didn't.

There was no blood it was just a daft bit of fun, but this boy was not happy. At lunchtime along with his friend they beat me up. I was punched and battered about the head and face. The boy's friend, who blackened one of my eyes, was murdered shortly after.

Along with his identical twin brother, the 15-year-old twins caused havoc for years in a housing scheme in Glasgow. Until a 20-year-old man came looking for apparently the other twin and stabbed the wrong twin to death. Maybe the killer did kill the wrong twin or maybe he was looking for any twin, or both twins.

The murderer was found guilty and jailed for life. He might have been a child killer, but the twins were able and fought men.

In Newfield I shared a room with another friend of the twin boys mentioned. My dad gave Danny a black suit to wear to the funeral of the murdered twin.

After the twin hit me in the Kibble, along with Danny, we ran away from our classes and got stoned in one of the closes in Shortroods.

We ran away loads of times until we got sent home for absconding during school hours and returning under the influence of drugs. The twin was taken home but me and Danny had to go back to our room in Newfield.

The twin was a decent boy, but he just wanted to fight with everyone and it cost him his life. Apparently, he was the quiet twin. Or maybe quieter.

Chapter 26

After taking the doing and being in the Kibble, I started going to boxing practice in order to be able to fight. In the Kibble, boys would fight all the time, but I couldn't fight so I went to boxing to learn how to.

By this time, I had worked my home leaves up to every night except one night per week. I was home six nights. I had to go to the Kibble every day for school, but I was home every night.

On school mornings I would get the same bus to Bridge of Weir with all the other children who went to Gryffe High School. I would get off at the bus stop at Bull's garage and then walk up to Gryffe Home and the staff would drive me to the Kibble in the van.

Until I was banned from the minibus for fighting with a member of staff while onboard.

I went to boxing classes two nights a week, but I wanted to get stoned every minute of every day. I would get stoned first thing in the morning and then go to school stoned and disappear out of the class for more hash.

I met a boy called Eggy who was from Paisley not far from where the school was. I smoked hash with him when we disappeared out of our classes. But Eggy wasn't in my class he was a year younger than me.

After things going so well, I ended up being arrested. Along with two boys, we were captured because we broke into the tennis court and the bowling club in Kilmacolm. It was the 1st of January 2000 which was the first day of the millennium. And we were taken to the Greenock Police Station for a few hours.

One of the two policemen who arrested us said that we were the worst housebreakers he had ever heard of. That is why we got caught because the neighbours heard us.

The other policeman was the bully and he said we were animals because one of the boys did a shit on the floor of the tennis club.

We never even managed to steal anything, not even a tennis racquet and we were captured because we made too much of a racket!

Chapter 27

By getting arrested and charged with two break-ins all my home leaves were stopped again. I was back to being kept in the Newfield seven nights a week.

After a while I worked my way back to getting more home leaves but before I got them all back the staff let me go to boxing. Then the boxing instructor moved to another venue, to a proper gym with a ring and better fighters so we had no instructor. But the man who ran the community centre left the doors open and we could train on most nights.

I was driven to boxing three nights a week. Due to smoking hash, I couldn't be bothered so I gave up boxing, but I still got the staff to run me and leave me there so that I could get stoned in Kilmacolm. I have never been in a boxing ring or had a proper fight. I packed it in because I wanted to get stoned every day.

My dad started boxing at three years of age. He trained in the same gym as Jim Watt who became world champion.

The Newfield staff told me that they would get me home after a number of months, but because I kept on re-offending on home leaves it took me a year to get back home.

After I turned 15, I was told I was going home. The Kibble said that I could still go there as a day boy, but I wanted to go back to the Mearns Centre in Greenock.

The summer holidays came and I went on holiday with my family to a caravan park in France. I met a girl and I was drinking pints of beer every night. Before I went on my holiday, I took half an ecstasy tablet and when I came back it wasn't long before I took a full one. I also experimented with acid (LSD). I tried these different drugs, but I always said that I would never try heroin.

My social worker came and left a written note on the stairwell of my house which read

'*Nathan doesn't have to go back to Newfield*'.

I could have cried with joy. I was back home at 15.

I came out of residential units early and I never got locked up in secure. I had won (*even though I got done for trying to fire a slug gun at someone*).

Chapter 28

I beat the system, but I had lost my education. I came out of care nine months sooner than the panel had set for me, but now I was a drug addict. I was hooked on hash. I smoked it every morning as soon as I opened my eyes. When I was 13 and 14, I wanted to get stoned but when I was 15, I knew I was trapped.

I went back into the Mearns Centre but I only lasted three months and then I got put out for fighting with a boy. I was moved to Unity Enterprise until I turned 16.

I got paid £1 a day for attending Unity Enterprise, five days a week. I also started signing on for bridging allowance once a fortnight at the Port Glasgow Job Centre (£30). I got a paper round delivering newspapers for the corner shop for £14 a week. I would collect my newspapers then smoke hash before delivering my round. Most mornings my dad drove me around in his car while I was stoned.

Along with another boy, we broke into an empty fruit shop in Kilmacolm and before the council got the place boarded up, I had taken the backdoor key. The old fruit shop was next door to a newspaper shop. Before I delivered my newspapers, I would smoke hash in the fruit shop then go round the doors delivering the newspapers. I was wasted every day at seven o'clock in the morning.

My life was getting stoned every day and getting spaced out at the weekend. My ambition at 15 was to leave day care at 16, get a giro so that I could get stoned all day every day. I was totally ignorant of my education and I had fallen into drugs at such a young age. Taking drugs was now my passion. Every penny I got went on drugs.

One day after Unity Enterprise, along with a boy called Lee (*and some others*) we went and got drunk in an empty house in Lyndoch Street, Greenock. It was a high-rise building and we were in a house up near the top floor. I am scared of heights, so I stayed away from the window.

Then after one of the boys finished his drink, he climbed out the window and was hanging off the top flat. I freaked out and ran out of the building with Lee. Luckily, the boy climbed back in and we saw him again at the bottom of the building.

Soon after this I was caught buzzing gas in Unity Enterprise. My dad came to pick me up and the leader of the project told him that he'd caught me inhaling gas from the tin which he took off me.

I later met a boy and he buzzed a tin of gas and it blew up in his face and killed him. It also set one of his girlfriend's arms on fire and she lost a hand. Tragic, as she was left on her own with their small child. I don't know if she gave up solvent abuse. Hopefully, this happening would make her stop. But she can still get a job working in a secondhand shop!

Chapter 29

At different times I would see girls from Port Glasgow in Kilmacolm. The police told me that when there's Port girls, there's Port boys and they were right. More or less every time there were Port girls, a crowd of these boys would appear and chase me up the street.

Every time I got caught, I would get beat up. I wasn't in any fights it was all one sided. I would get punched and kicked about. Even though I had done boxing, whenever I got attacked it would all happen that fast I would either get punched about or I would run away.

After getting battered every time violence came my way, I wanted to hurt the boys who were going to start with me. I was smoking hash every single day, dependent on it, was watching violent movies all the time and getting drunk at the weekends.

I took my big sister's hockey stick and I carried it with me down my tracksuit trousers everywhere I went in case Port boys came looking for me.

I have been chased from crowds of up to 10 to 15 boys and more. I ran away time and time again. I have been chased back from Port Glasgow to Kilmacolm, running all the way back along the fields. And I started to regret running away all the time.

I had just come out of a bad boy's school and the boys who wanted to batter me hadn't. They all went to mainstream schools and I had just come out of the Kibble. This made me think that I could be worse than all of them.

One night a crowd of boys came looking for me to beat me up. I ran at them, determined to hit one of them with the hockey stick but they all ran away and I chased after them. A boy tried to hit me with a bit of wood, but I managed to get it off him. I chased him on to the cycle track and he ran home.

I realised that they weren't coming to fight with me, they were coming to beat me up. This was the same as me not fighting back, just taking a beating. These boys now knew that I was wanting to hurt them.

On Halloween 2000 I was standing at the Cross when the Greenock bus pulled up. The passengers all emptied on to the street and there were about 40 boys or maybe more. They chased me home and surrounded my house, standing outside my building making a ruckus.

In the next few months (*before I turned 16*) I ended up with every single 'young team' in Port Glasgow after me. They would all join up to come and batter me. They would chase me and I would chase them and I was punched and kicked about the streets of Kilmacolm. I was also hit with wooden sticks and glass bottles.

At the weekends I would drink my bottle of Buckfast and then keep the empty bottle up my sleeve in case anyone came near me. I carried a small wooden baseball bat up my sleeve as well. I would carry glass bottles and I stole a spiked dog collar from the pet shop in Greenock. Sometimes I would wear jeans so that I could attach a leather belt with a tough metal buckle so that I could whip it off and swing it. It wasn't a fashion contest, the bigger and harder the better.

I got involved in what can only be described as recreational violence. I was on my own. I had no one to help me fight the Port boys. Everyone I was with would run away and if I stood my ground I would get beaten up. Kilmacolm didn't have a gang so I created the *Young Kilma Derry* and it was just me. I met a boy called Wilky. He was supposed to stab me, but we went home for tea.

Chapter 30

I created a nickname for myself and spray painted it all over Kilmacolm. **Conza** was written everywhere by me. Then a notice appeared in the Kilmacolm newspaper saying, 'who is Conza'?

The whole point of this notice was written about me but not to me. It was to shame my parents by saying that previously dog owners in Kilmacolm had been asked to clean up their dog's mess so why shouldn't the parents of Conza clean up his mess. So out of guilt and doing the admirable thing, my dad went out in the middle of the night wearing a dark hooded top over his head with a tub of paint and a brush and painted over all my mentions.

How would that have looked if my dad had been caught by police? Everyone would think that he was Conza!

I longed for Kilmacolm to have a gang which I could be a member of, but there was never a crowd of boys who were willing to fight. Although, this didn't stop me wishing there was. I would graffiti 'KYT' all over the Cross and other parts of Kilmacolm. I created a theme that Kilmacolm did have a young team (*which was my dream*).

Chapter 31

I was high on Buckfast and ecstasy and the police came to lift me for smashing a car up. As soon as they came into my house, I opened my kitchen window and climbed out onto the roof. In Kilmacolm my family home was the top flat, up a stairwell close. Three houses in the one building and we lived up the top.

I told the police that I would only come down if they gave me a policeman's belt. I told them to give it to my wee brother and he would keep it for me. One of the policemen took off his police belt and gave it to my wee brother and Benny went down the stairs with it.

I could see my brother from on high standing outside our building holding my police belt. I shouted down at him telling him to *"keep it for me"* but all the police surrounded my brother and took the belt from him. I missed out on asking for the handcuffs and the CS gas (pepper spray) and obviously the police baton!

After about an hour, I got fed up, so I came back in and I was arrested. I was still only 15 but the police kept me in overnight for an emergency panel the next day but at the Children's Hearing I was let back out.

There was talk at this panel again of me being put in secure. The hearing members said they weren't sure if I should be locked up in a children's secure unit until I turned 16. They said that residential school didn't work but Newfield and the approved school did work (Kibble), but I still wasn't 16 so there was talk of me being locked up until I turned that age.

The panel decided to send me to a children's hospital in Dumfries for another mental assessment, but I refused to go back after I visited it. I was also sent to Yorkhill Hospital, but I refused to go back in the second time. I sat in my mum's car. The doctor came out to see me whilst I was outside in the car park. I refused to go inside the hospital because the first time I went there were people watching me through a glass screen, which freaked me out.

When I got arrested for climbing up on to my house roof, the police said that I held a siege. When I needed the toilet, I urinated off the roof hoping to hit some of the officers who were standing below me. I never had any success. I pissed and missed!

Chapter 32

B ecause of my criminal behaviour (*when I was supposed to be in residential care*) I was put into a group called the Gap Project. I did modules with other boys and girls for our offending behaviour. The staff who worked at the Gap were probation officers. The courts sent accused persons over 16 to probation and the panel sent me to the Gap Project, which was ran by the same staff, where we did roughly the same group work. This was where social workers put you if it looked like you were going to jail. Most of us did in fact end up in prison.

I met three boys from Port Glasgow. They didn't want to fight with me and I didn't want to fight with them, I liked them from the start. Patman, Dunga and 'D' used to come to Kilmacolm every night and they would either come in for me or I would see them about the Cross. 'D' and Dunga were best friends. They did everything together they were inseparable.

Over the next few months, me and Patman became quite close and we were together most days and he would often stay overnight with me in my family home. One day we found an empty caravan on the grounds of my old Pastor's house (*where the Wendy hut was*). The caravan wasn't locked so we went in and sat inside. We would all sit in there, drink and smoke hash. Me and Patman even stayed in it for the odd night over the weekend and nights here and there. The caravan was our gang's gaff until boys from the Port smashed it up. After we lost the caravan, I put a sofa in a shed in my garden and used it to smoke weed and drink in it with people.

One day Patman came and asked me if I wanted to go and stay at his gran's with him. She was away somewhere for a few days, so we had the house to ourselves. Patman treated me to a king kebab then I suggested that we get drunk.

We went over to Tesco's and made our way to the alcohol section, but there was no Buckfast on any of the shelves, so I grabbed a bottle of After Shock and stuck it up my sleeve and then we tried to exit the shop.

We didn't get far before we were both huckled at the front door. We were then carted to a room to wait on the police arriving. I had helped myself to sweets in the shop and to show off to Patman I began eating them. Also, in an attempt to swallow the evidence.

The police came and arrested us and we were taken to the Greenock Police Station. When I was asked my name, I lied about my identity, but the duty officer knew me from Kilmacolm and I was told who I really was.

My dad refused to come and get me and Patman's gran was away, so the police took us both to Crosshill Children's Home in Port Glasgow. The police marched us both in and removed the handcuffs. A member of staff then took us from the police and showed us to our rooms.

When we got to the sleeping area, Patman asked if we could share a room, but the staff told us that this wasn't allowed. So, I did an old trick that I had done in Dundee. I made a run for it and with Patman we both ran out the fire exit.

The police officers were still in the office (*with whoever was in charge of the home*) while we ran past the police car that was parked outside. We then walked all the way to Greenock in the middle of the night eating stolen sweets.

The next day we went to Kilmacolm where the police arrested us and tried to take us back to Crosshill, but they wouldn't accept us, so we were both taken home.

I didn't have to go back to the Crosshill Children's Unit. After a short while Patman was taken back for about a week. I was only in that home for about fifteen seconds. I walked in one door and back out the other with my brother to another mother.

Chapter 33

A friend from Port Glasgow started going joy riding and stealing cars and I wanted to do it as well. Then one day I was walking up my street when I noticed that there was a wee Fiesta parked with the keys still in the door. As quick as you like I took the keys from outside the car and I took them up the road with me. I couldn't drive but I told a boy I met about having the car keys and he told me he was the best car thief in Port Glasgow. I gave him the car keys and he took the car for me.

I waited around the corner for him to pick me up in the stolen car. Suddenly, I heard a car screeching and I knew it was him coming to get me. When he picked me up, he drove along the street and he told me that there was a full tank of petrol. This convinced him that whoever the owner was, he/she intended someone to steal the car and drive far. Not even a mile later the driver stalled the car and froze.

He started the ignition and tried to take off but stalled the car again and again. He kept turning the engine off and on again trying to drive off, but he stalled the car about 20 times. Adam was in the car as well and suddenly we realised that the driver was not as good a car thief as he'd told us. We both laughed while he screamed at us to get out and push. So, me and Adam got out the car and pushed with the driver screaming at us to push harder. Then he managed to accelerate and took off and started driving again. He had to stop though to let us get back in. The driver told us that he couldn't get the car in gear, then he drove us about all day. We were pushing at the rear so he could steer. He said he was the best car thief in the Port and couldn't get the car into gear!

Chapter 34

I hadn't seen Patman for a few months then he came back to Kilmacolm one night and I went with him to his new house in Greenock. Then I started going to his house every week. After the Gap Project on a Thursday, I would get a bottle of Buckfast from Lyndoch Street, then walk up to Kenilworth Crescent with my bottle. I would stay in Patman's at the weekend most weekends.

Kenilworth was a ghetto in Greenock. I knew I was in a rough place. When I was in Newfield and Kibble, I liked the other boys, who were from rough and dangerous areas, so I felt excited about staying in a rundown slum.

I was in the Gap Project with other boys who had been charged with attempted murder by stabbing guys. They were out on bail and were facing going to jail and a boy I met called Wilky, was in a secure unit doing four years for stabbing a guy in Kenilworth. This inspired me and made me wish that I had stabbed someone. I wanted to do it.

Round about this same time I started getting death threats. A man in his 30s was nearly killed on my street at the Kilmacolm Cross and everyone said that it was me. The police were looking for an attempted murderer. I was never charged or even questioned, but one day on a bus a man told me he was going to cut my throat. Guys were phoning up my family home and leaving voice messages in the middle of the night telling me and my family that I was getting killed. I got threatening voicemails on my mobile phone and horrible text messages sent as well.

The man I am talking about got knocked clean out at the Kilmacolm Cross one Saturday night and he had to be taken to hospital by ambulance. People were saying that I smashed his face in with a bottle and that I was stamping on his head. I also heard that I was meant to have hit him with a metal bar. But I can assure you that I had done none of these things to this man. I was told that the man was in a coma and nearly died and over a year later I heard that he got nine thousand pounds compensation because he was left deaf in one ear. In my innocence no-one's going to clear me. If I had attempted to murder him I would apologise, but what's the point? He won't be able to hear me.

Chapter 35

Now I was known in Kilmacolm and Port Glasgow for nearly killing a man and meanwhile I was in the Gap Project in Greenock every week with other boys who had been charged with attempted murder. They used knives and this did inspire me.

One day I went to the Gap Project and because I was 16, I was asked if I wanted to go to a movie audition, but I never went. All the other boys were only 15 but I had turned 16 first and the film that was being made in Greenock was called *Sweet 16*. I heard the camera crew were in Kenilworth filming.

In later years, my brother went to Amsterdam to watch Celtic play Ajax and he met the films leading star and got a photograph taken with him.

Now that I was 16 years old my benefits went up in price. I started signing on for £84 a fortnight. I was claiming job seeker's allowance, but I wasn't seeking a job and all my money went on drink and drugs.

Patman gave his house up and moved to Port Glasgow, but I didn't want to leave the scheme, so I went to the housing offices and signed on the waiting list for a house in Kenilworth.

Before he left Kenilworth, Patman started selling drugs and Adam started hanging about with him.

Patman moved to Port Glasgow's Clune Park Street and Adam got a flat in the same building as him.

Patman has a heart of gold. He made a fortune selling cannabis resin and marijuana and he remained loyal and generous with his money. Although Adam was never to know, Patman was going to make plenty selling pot (*he hit the jackpot*).

Chapter 36

Since I was 13, I drank every Friday and Saturday and then I started drinking on a Sunday as well. I stopped going to Church, I just got drunk instead. When I got sent to Parkview, I ran away all the time and drank every other day. Then when I went into Newfield I didn't drink as much but I smoked hash most days in there. When I came out of Newfield, I started drinking three or four days out of every week.

At the Gap Project I did group work which was for a few days each week. After I finished all the modules, I had to attend every Thursday and I started drinking after that with Lee. Lee was also in Unity Enterprise with me. He liked a drink the same as I did. I drank myself too. I was 15 and I drank most days out of every week.

Kibble was a rough school but that was my past and I even wished now that I had been in secure. I wanted to be a bad boy. I was 16 and I wanted to use a knife on someone. I wanted some form of notoriety.

I had been in stolen cars, but I was only a passenger. Then on my 17th birthday my granda taught me how to drive. He only took me out twice because I was addicted to hash, so my heart wasn't in it. I got drunk most days as well. I gave up learning to drive with my granda as my instructor but by now I knew the basics.

A few weeks later I ended up in prison. I was full of Buckfast and valium and I chased a guy around the football pitch at the Birkmyre Park in Kilmacolm with a knife. I was arrested with Dave.

We spent the night in Greenock Police Station, then were taken to court the next day. We were put in the court cells at the Greenock Sheriff Court. That was when I first got my lawyer (*18 June 2002*).

When I was arrested, I wasn't searched properly and the police never found my knife, so I managed to conceal it down my trousers. The first ever time I went into the court cells I had a blade on me.

My lawyer told me I would get out, but I needed a bail address. But I didn't have one. I had been kicked out of my house. So, when we went up to court, I got a shut eye with a bang. I was sent to prison. The real jail, not the police station. I got remanded for three weeks because I was NFA (*no fixed abode*).

Before I left the court cells, I gave my knife to an institutionalised prisoner and he disposed of it for me. I was then searched and taken to prison. In my attempt to get out I failed. Dave got bailed and I got jailed.

Chapter 37

I was taken to HMP Greenock which was known locally as Gateside. I was put in Ailsa Hall. I was kept on suicide watch because it was my first time in jail and I had tried to kill myself when I was 13.

When the mental health team is involved and you've attempted suicide, whenever you go into jail the nurses and doctors make the decision above the prison wardens. I was cheeky and threatened a screw, so I was stripped naked and put in a suicide suit and threw in a bare cell with nothing. On my first ever night in jail, I was lying on a mat on the floor with a pair of padded shorts and a t-shirt on. There were no sheets on the mat, no duvet cover over the quilt and no pillow. There were no curtains on the window in the cell. It was a horrible first night in jail and I had over three weeks to face. The next day I knew not to be cheeky, so I was moved into another cell with a proper jail bed, bedding and a television.

The screws told me that I was getting out the next day, that I had been given a bail address and my lawyer had got me another court date. The screws asked me if I knew any of the other prisoners and they would ask one of them if he wanted to come into the observation cell with me to keep me company for the night.

I had read in the newspaper that a boy I knew from the Mearns Centre was in. When I told the screws about him, they told me that he was on protection. The screws then asked me for the second time if I wanted to go on protection, but I refused again.

When I went into Gateside, the screws asked me if I needed to be protected in the prison and I said **No**. When I saw the doctor and the nurse, because it was my first time in jail and I had previously tried to end it all at such a young age they put me on observation.

This other guy I knew was on protection, but the screws asked him if he wanted to come into the suicide cell with me and he agreed to come in. There was a camera in the cell with a window where the screw sits in his office.

So, I shared a cell with him for a night *(and without even realising, I made a complete fool of myself)*. Even though this guy was on protection they still put him in with me. In any other jail that I've known, if another prisoner is on protection then they don't mix with mainstream prisoners.

This was my first time in and I was kept in two different suicide cells for both nights. Protection in Gateside just means that you are kept down the bottom flat and you don't mix with other prisoners. I was kept down the bottom flat with all the other protection cases because I was on suicide watch and it was my first-time in.

The next day I got out of Gateside after only a couple of days and I now knew not to give the prison wardens any cheek. I call my first time in jail a sneak peek because I got out after two days *(not 3 weeks)*.

Chapter 38

I was homeless. I couldn't stay at my bail address it was just a ploy to get me out. I'd been thrown out of my mum and dad's house, so I had to go to the homeless centre. I asked for a house in Kenilworth, but I was put into the Inverclyde Centre, a homeless hostel in Greenock.

I kept my head down but a few weeks later another man was put into the same flat as me. When I wasn't in, he ate all my food and drank all my juice. So, I flew at him with a shovel. He ran out of our flat and I gathered all his belongings and put them out the front door. When I was packing his stuff, I found a bag full of needles and syringes. I opened the door and I threw them out at him.

On different Sundays, the police would contact the hostel to arrange for a few of the males to go over to the police station for an ID parade. I only went once and I was told never to come back because I was cheeky, but the police paid me £10.

Then a boy I'd met in the centre stole a tenner from me and I was then banned for life because I was fighting with him in and around the hostel. We both smashed bottles off each other's heads. I was barred but he wasn't. I later saw the boy I was fighting with on the Trisha Show.

I was still homeless but barred from the homeless hostel, so the Greenock Council had no choice but to offer me a house quicker than I would have had to wait if I had kept my head down in the Inverclyde Centre. I was told the only other option was for them to put me into a hotel somewhere which would have cost them money. There were loads of empty houses in Kenilworth.

I went into the housing offices with my girlfriend where I was offered the choice of two houses. When we were told the addresses we both laughed because my girlfriend stayed in one of the buildings. I picked the house, to live in my girlfriend's close. The other building had been done up and refurbished but I wanted to live in the rougher close.

I was leaving Kilmacolm, the millionaire capital of Scotland to move to the biggest ghetto in Greenock. I wanted to live in a rundown house in a rundown area. To me it wasn't that bad at all because it's what I wanted.

Before I got my flat, I took my girlfriend's younger brother to the cinema to watch Star Wars – Attack of The Clones. He was about eight years old and after the movie finished, I offered to buy him a Star Wars toy, but he asked me to get him a baseball bat instead. So, to humour him, I bought him one. The wooden bat came with a soft ball, but he wasn't interested in the ball at all, he only wanted the bat to carry as a weapon. I noticed that the children who hung around Kenilworth didn't play with toys. They smashed windows and gathered sticks. The only toys that I ever saw them with was a cosh. Because I was from Kilmacolm people thought that I was posh and had lots of dosh.

Chapter 39

Along with my family, we were all going on holiday to Florida for three weeks. I was more excited about getting my own flat in Greenock (*when I came back from America*) than I was about going on my holiday of a lifetime to USA. I was with my family in the Glasgow airport for three hours waiting on our flight and all I could think about was hash. When we landed, I got off the plane and started shouting and screaming at my mum and dad. I blamed them for taking me to America. I was so angry; I could have cried. I was walking around the Florida airport screaming. I was lucky the armed police never shot me, then jailed me.

For the full three weeks in Florida, I couldn't get to sleep at all. Every night I was up until the sun came out, smoking cigarettes. I never even went to all the theme parks with my family. I stayed in the apartment drinking beer by myself. We all went out every evening for a meal and I had a cooked steak (*well done*) every single night. I was getting bigger and bigger steaks after my dad was sure I could eat them, after he saw me devour a smaller one the night before. I knew when I came back home, I was going to get a big bit of hash and a bottle of Buckfast instead of beers.

As soon as I got back to Kilmacolm, I went and bought a bottle of Buckfast and a half ounce of hash and I was happy. Two days later I went into the housing offices and picked up the keys to my house in Greenock. That night I moved into 5 Hole Farm Road with nothing. I had everything I could want at my family home, but I left there for this. I had my bit of hash and a kitchen devil. The thoughts that I had were rife and I wanted to do more than strife. I slept with the knife.

Chapter 40

Within about a week a deep feeling of fear and terror came over me. I went totally paranoid. I thought that all the

Port boys that I'd fought with in Kilmacolm would come to my flat looking for me. I moved to Greenock because I wanted to make a name for myself and I became a nervous, paranoid wreck within days. I was terrified.

The next morning, I walked down to the shop and bought a bottle of Buckfast. I was only 17 *(too young to get legally served)* the woman who served me called me baby face. The paranoia was screaming out of me, but I couldn't stop smoking hash, which was doing this to me. I was totally obsessed with cannabis. It felt like I would never be able to get off it. So, I started drinking every morning to try and take away the paranoia, but I was still smoking hash on top which didn't really work. I loved Buckfast so I became a daily drinker.

After I'd been signing on for a year on Job Seeker's Allowance, the Job Centre wanted me to get a job, but I didn't want to work. I couldn't have held down a job anyway due to my addiction, so my Career's Adviser told me that I'd be better to get a sick line. If I didn't, I would be getting cut off my benefit because it was obvious, I had no intentions of working. I went to the doctor and got a six-week sick line for drug abuse. I now got £140 a fortnight. When I went back to the Health Centre, I got a further 12-week sick line.

In Kilmacolm, I stole a meat clever out my dead neighbour's house. My mum had the house keys after the old man had died and I helped myself to his keys and fetched the chopper.

I started getting valium cheap and I would buy 50 or 100 at a time. Valium hit you for days and I was drinking every morning and smoking hash buckets. I was in a terrible state and mixing Buckfast with valium, you get trouble.

I collected knives since I was 13 and now, I gathered different weapons. I kept them all in my flat. I had a meat cleaver, hatchet, kitchen knife, metal bar and two baseball bats.

The paranoia messed my head up and I was living a life that felt like mental agony. I would sleep with a knife under my pillow. I surrounded myself with dangerous weapons all around my bed while I was asleep.

Some nights I would hear people outside my flat talking about me. I could hear my letterbox opening and voices talking about coming through my door to get me. Then one night I was full of valium and I ran out with a boiling hot kettle to scold whoever I found outside. This time I didn't care but there wasn't even anyone there. My paranoia was giving me a scare.

Chapter 41

Most of the teenagers in Kenilworth used to hang around the different buildings smoking hash. I met these youngsters and from that point on they never sat in the closes, they all came to my house. Every night without fail my flat would be full of boys and girls from Greenock. At first, I liked it but then I got fed up because I never had a moments peace. There was a Community Centre in Kenilworth but now my flat was the centre for all the Kenilworth young team. After a number of weeks, I realised that my house had been taken over. My flat became a local drink and drugs club for teenagers. The only club I wanted was a wooden one.

One night I was watching the television when adverts came on. I then saw a clip that the first ever showing of **A Clockwork Orange** was about to be shown on British television (2002) since it had been banned in 1971. Stanley Kubrick had died and the movie was no longer banned. I was very excited. I had tried to get my hands on a copy when I was in high school but failed. I was buzzing all week waiting for the film to come on that Sunday night at 10 o'clock.

I watched this movie while I recorded it. This film is evil, but I loved most of it. The next day which was Monday I went to the shop for my bottle. I returned to my flat and watched this demonic film as I drank my Buckfast. When the film finished, I rewound the tape and watched it again. I watched it over and over, for many days I watched it repeatedly. I must have been sickening everyone else in my house making them watch it day in and day out but not as much as I was sickening myself inside. I never asked any of them to constantly be in my flat with me. Along with the Buckfast and valium in my system, this film wired me. Very quickly I became obsessed with **Clockwork Orange**.

My world was now turned upside down. I wanted to knife someone and get caught to look evil. I wanted everyone to think I was mental. I fantasised about being infamous. I moved to Greenock because I wanted to make a name for myself. Now I wanted to mutilate someone. I was sick. The cannabis did make me paranoid, but I also knew what I was doing. I wasn't mad, I was bad and I was glad (*how sad*).

Chapter 42

On the early hours of Saturday 26th October 2002, I was arrested and charged with attempted murder. I attacked an 18-year-old boy in the living room of my house. I made no effort to get away. After I did it, I left my flat and waited in the close for the police to come and get me.

That night my mum was working night shift in the hospital where the boy was taken. The next day on her way home she drove by Kenilworth. On her way along Hole Farm Road she noticed the police were coming out of my flat carrying a long metal bar in an evidence bag.

I slashed the boy on his face and I hit him on the head with a metal bar. The police had the metal bar, my clothes which were covered in blood and they had me. As soon as the officers got me to the police station, they stripped me naked and took all my clothes for forensic DNA evidence. My clothes were taken off me and I was given a white forensic suit to wear in the cell. I lay on a mat in the Greenock Police Station and I didn't know how long I was going to jail for.

Later that day, I was taken upstairs and the CID charged me with attempted murder. I now had regrets and I tried to lie my way out of it, but I was still charged. At least my victim never died so I knew I would not be going to jail until I was a man.

My victim did not deserve this, but he was cheeky and refused to give me an ecstasy tablet then he gave my girlfriend one instead. He was brought to my flat by his friend who acted the hardman every week and then became a witness against me.

My solicitor came to see me while I was being held in the police station. He asked me if I did it and I told him that I had. I then asked him how long I was going to prison for?

I only lasted two months in Greenock before I was arrested for an attempted murder in the living room of my house. The paranoia disturbed me and I made myself live in a violent atmosphere. I was now full of fear when my lawyer told me I was going to get jailed for eight years.

Chapter 43

On the Monday I was taken in a police van to Greenock Sheriff Court and I was locked in the cells with Dunga and his friend. Dunga's friend was in for a driving offence and Dunga was his best friend, art & part. I was due to appear at court on that day anyway for chasing a guy with a knife in Kilmacolm. So now I would have two court appearances on that day.

Before I went up to any courts, I was taken to see my lawyer where I found out there was good news and bad news. The good news was that the charge had been reduced from attempted murder to danger of life and the bad news was I was going to jail that day to start my years. I wasn't facing eight years anymore now it was six. Because I had broken bail conditions, I was going to jail. Now I was in a hole and I wanted to make it even deeper. I was full of regret. I spoke to my lawyer just before 10 o'clock in the morning and he told me I would be appearing in private first, because I was charged with a very serious offence. I would be appearing in private, so no one would be in the court's gallery. On my second appearance I would be appearing in an open court.

A while later, the cell door was opened up and I was handcuffed to a police officer and marched into the courtroom. I was remanded in custody and I was told to expect six years in jail. Now I had nothing to lose.

I was put back in the cell, waiting to go to jail, but first I had to wait on my other court appearance. Dunga and his friend both got remanded as well. When the police came and opened the cell door to take me back to court and my name was shouted, I was to get handcuffed and taken back up to court.

I stripped off all my clothes and walked out the cell door totally naked. The policeman had the handcuffs round one of his hands wanting to cuff me to him, but he changed his mind. He took the handcuffs off his hand and put them on me and then cuffed them. Then this policeman marched me up to court pulling me by the handcuffs.

This time I was not appearing in private, this was an open court, so I knew there would be people in the court gallery. When I heard my name being called the policeman opened the court door and said to the judge, "the prisoner wishes to come in to court, as he is,". The judge must have thought I was drunk on drugs, something that happens every day, so he just ordered me in. I walked into court as naked as the day I was born.

There weren't many people in the court gallery. My dad, my co-accused and his mum were there. I had been remanded in custody a while before and had been told I was going to jail for six years so, I fought back and made out that I didn't care anymore. I wanted everyone to think that I was mad anyway.

The judge, the PF and my lawyer were all laughing and so were all the police, but I wasn't. The judge ordered a mental health examination for bizarre behaviour in court, as he laughed his head off. All the court workers were laughing as well as they did their courtroom duties. I was taken back down to the cell underneath the courts.

It was 28th of October 2002 which was 'D's' 18th birthday and he was sent to jail laughing his head off, saying that I had given him a happy birthday. I waited until I was in an open court, I didn't want to flash my privates in private. Some people thought I was a freak because after I got remanded for a week I decided to streak.

Chapter 44

I walked into Gateside Prison, then I was given three valium. Real diazepam, not like the ones I was taking on the streets. I was given a detox because I had valium in my system and I was glad. I was put back on suicide watch again for another two days. Then I was moved up the stairs to the second flat in Ailsa Hall. At nighttime, I was given another three blues. I got some hash and smoked it and I was wrecked. I was given three blue valium in the morning and three at night. A boy I was in Kibble with was getting his girlfriend to smuggle hash in and he gave me some every day. I was wrecked for the week in jail.

After my seven-day remand I was taken back to court and I was remanded for a further 110 days. Because I appeared naked in the dock a week before and the fact I had ADHD, the judge sent me to Dykebar Psychiatric Hospital in Paisley for an assessment. I was fully committed and mentally committed at the same time.

Before I was taken to Dykebar, the police accused me of stabbing another 17-year-old boy in the court cells. The boy told the police I stabbed him on the head with a pen. This was the same boy who I had shared a cell with for the night, he was on protection (*but I wasn't*). The court cell was covered in blood. I told the police that the boy fell and split his head on the bench and was dripping blood all over the floor and walls. I was searched and the officers found my pen and confiscated it for forensic examination, but it had not been used to hurt him. One officer said, "Well done".

Before they let this boy out the court cell, he told the police I left him for dead. Then he went home via the hospital to get staples in his head.

Chapter 45

When the police took me to Dykebar, they told the nurses that I had just stabbed a boy in the court cells. It was the same officers who knew me from climbing up on my mum's rooftop. They warned the nurses in case I went up on the hospital roof.

I asked for valium, but I was given a dose of chlorpromazine (*largactil*). It was liquid medicine and it was good stuff. I got a buzz off it and I quite liked this medication. So, I got a good night's sleep that first night in Dykebar.

Then the next day I wasn't given anything in the morning so I couldn't sleep that Tuesday night. Then on Wednesday, I wouldn't get up out my bed in the morning. The nurses tried to get me up, but I refused. I told them I would only get up if they gave me valium. They told me that if I got up, I would get valium. I got up but they never gave me any, so I went back to bed.

Then they dragged me up and threw me to my feet. I became really aggressive and threatened the nurses. So, they jumped on me and restrained me. They lay on top of me holding me down for about 30 minutes. When they let me up, they sat me down on a chair where I sat for five days with members of staff.

Monday came and the police took me back to the Greenock Court where I was put in a cell on my own, because now I was a mental patient. I wanted to go back to jail but the judge never sent me back to prison. He sectioned me again for another three months. No-one would listen to me complain. For 12 weeks I was to remain in the lunatic asylum for the criminally insane.

Chapter 46

I was in the back of a police van, which pulled up at the big gate at Carstairs and my heart sank. The police were waiting outside for about half an hour with me in the back. My belongings were handed over with my possessions and all my stuff was searched while I was waiting.

Then the gate opened, we drove in and my nightmare began. I was to stay here to be assessed for 12 weeks over the festive period and it was a real-life nightmare before Christmas.

The police van drove through the whole hospital then pulled up at Lomond Ward. The police parked outside and one of the officers got out of the van and rang the doorbell. Two minutes later a woman came and opened the door. Then I was taken inside.

I still had handcuffs on and the police were carting me into this hospital. The nurses took me into a room and asked the police to take the handcuffs off. They were two big men about 18 stone wearing black trousers and white shirts. I asked to phone my mum, but they wouldn't let me, so I huffed and puffed. The two big nurses jumped on me pulling me to the ground. And I was restrained for about an hour. Meanwhile an alarm rang out bellowing 'send staff to Lomond, send staff to Lomond'.

These two big heavies were lying on top of me holding me down twisting my wrists back. They were torturing me and then one of the nurses started to whisper in my ear, "you are a little shit, you are in the state hospital now and you are nothing".

I heard the police running back into the room and asking the nurses if they wanted them to put the handcuffs back on, but the nurses said the handcuffs weren't needed. Obviously, they were used to this and I was nothing.

I burst out crying. Not loud but pretty hysterically. I had my face down on the carpet with these two big heavies on top of me deliberately hurting me. So, I cried and cried for a good 20 minutes. After they stopped restraining me my wrists were in agony. I could hear all the staff around me shouting at me telling me to calm down. I was broken and I was very scared.

I was three man teamed through the ward into another room with big mattresses on the floor and I was thrown onto one of the mats and restrained again. I was then told to lie on these mats. I had stopped crying. I had cried all I could, well I thought I had. Then they put me in a shower and they waved a metal detector around my entire naked body. I was told that I was on level 3s, which meant I had to have a member of staff with me, sitting beside me at all times. Even at nighttime my cell door was kept open with two members of staff sitting at the foot of my doorway talking all night. I had to lie on a mat on the floor and when I went for a shower (*and to the toilet*) a member of staff was in with me. I'd been in two weeks and I had to say my prayers because now I was taken to Carstairs.

Chapter 47

Remember, I was only 17 years old and I was put into the ward that assessed the male criminal lunatics in Scotland. When I got sent from the dock at the Greenock Court to Carstairs, the police officer that I was handcuffed to was from Kilmacolm. He was on the television programme, **Who Wants To Be A Millionaire** where he won £32000.

His son was in my class at primary and had stayed on after his exams and was still at high school. I wanted to achieve notoriety and I ended up in Carstairs at 17. I could have been a school pupil, but I was classed a high-risk criminal lunatic in the State Hospital.

After five days they took me off level 3s but before they did I had one of the male nurses who had retrained me, sitting next to me for a few hours and he would whisper in my ear, telling me that if I moved I would hit the carpet and he would jump on me. He was a sadistic pig.

I was only in this horrible place for two days and I realised how Carstairs is run. Through bullying tactics. If you step out of line you will get swung all over the place and pumped full of medication. All the patients are made (*no matter how mentally ill*) to sit there calm or they will get terrorised. If they tell you that you are taking medication and you don't take it, they will force feed you it. I don't mean orally; they will forcibly inject you with horrible drugs to take away your ability to think for yourself. I saw the staff play mind games with the patients.

Most days the assessment ward had activities. We were taken to the gym to play football or mostly volleyball. I hadn't played much football since primary school but in Carstairs I played again. Carstairs had a small shop on the grounds of the hospital and once a week we were taken to the shop to get cigarettes, sweeties and crisps etc. In the shop there was a library and a small cinema screen, where the ward would go once a week to watch a movie. I watched different films every week on the screen but really there was only one film that I wanted to see. So, I got my mum to bring it in from my collection. The whole ward would sit and watch the film over and over, even the nurses would watch it with us repeatedly. The film was one of the best (*One Flew Over The Cuckoo's Nest*)!

Chapter 48

My young sister was too young to come into the ward to visit me, so I had to go to the Family Centre to see her. At a family visit, I met a man who seemed alright but was deemed insane twice. He murdered a policeman in Glasgow and was declared insane and sectioned without limit of time. Then after recovering he was recharged and was presented as diminished responsibility for the second time. He was sectioned without limit of time, again. After a few years he got out.

There was a man in Lomond Ward with me, who along with his two co-accused, were the first people in Scotland to be convicted of murder without the police having found their victim's body. Still to this day the man they shot has never been found. The man in the ward's brother was the manager of Partick Thistle Football Club. I saw him up in the visit room.

One day all the patients in the ward started watching a football game. It was Celtic who were playing and before they start their games the Celtic players do what they call the 'huddle' and this one guy thought that the team were talking about him.

I met a man who had been in Carstairs for years because he held two women hostage in the Chunky Chicken Factory in Glasgow. He told the police that he would only let them go if he got a Michael Jackson costume. He was then deemed insane and sent to Carstairs doing the moonwalk. He told his hostages he was 'worse than the devil' and he told the nurses in Carstairs, he was satan himself.

Many years later (*on the day that Michael Jackson died*) the chunky chicken man phoned me from Carstairs and I asked him if he was gutted his favourite singer had died. He said, "It's a bit of a shock to the system, know". I wonder if the brute ever got his Michael Jackson suit?

Chapter 49

Being in the State Hospital I have seen insanity at its very peak. Carstairs is a place of madness. And it's madness with a capital M. The patients are one of four types of '**Ms**' (*Mongo, Monster, Maniac, Mental*).

I shouldn't have been a patient inside this place. I wouldn't say that I was any of these types of people. Going up to court naked was a stunt that went wrong and then because of my aggressive behaviour in Dykebar, it landed me in this top security loony bin. I wanted people to think that I was mad, so I went to court naked but after getting landed in Carstairs I very quickly changed my mind.

(1) Mongos are simple-minded.

(2) Monsters are the most evil, they have killed children or done other stuff to them.

(3) Maniacs just want to get out and take drugs while they are in.

(4) Mental people are capable of any bizarre behaviours and crimes.

Some of the mongos are monsters too and some of the mentals are everything that I have listed. Some maniacs are faking mental illnesses. They have lied and fooled nurses and doctors claiming to be mentally ill but in doing this they do have personality disorders. Most people don't like jail, but some feeble-minded prisoners pretend to be mental to avoid serving prison sentences. They can't handle the jail and, in my opinion, if you do the crime you do the time.

A patient offered me heroin and I told him that I wasn't a junkie, but he replied neither was he. He also told me not to tell any of the loons that he had smack, so I assured him that I wouldn't. I felt disgusted that I was offered it, but when I went to my bed for the night the devil came into me and I started thinking about taking heroin. I was broken being in Carstairs at 17 so I let my guard down and the next day I got a bag of smack. That night I snorted half in my cell and 10 minutes later I was out my face for hours. I was wrecked. Before the sun came up, I snorted the other half and when my door was opened for a shower I went and lay in the bath zonked.

When I went to breakfast, I was still out my face and I smoked a cigarette and it made me feel even more smashed. Then the guy who gave me it, gave me another rollup cigarette with heroin in it. I smoked it and was blasted out my face for most of the day.

This was my introduction to heroin, from a patient in Carstairs. This guy was kept for years and then got out and died young. I always said that I would never take smack and now I did. Before I got locked up, I went paranoid because of the hash that I was smoking. Then while I was a patient in Carstairs I was worried that they might keep my inside for years. So now I had to prove that there wasn't anything wrong with me.

After being in for six weeks it was Christmas. I woke up on Christmas day 2002 in Carstairs. I got a nice turkey dinner and my mum and dad came to visit me. I was broken. I was even given a Christmas present from all the staff at the State Mental Hospital which was a Lynx Africa Box Set with a shower gel. There was no deodorant but there was a talking clock.

I think Carstairs is one of the only places that would have any use for a talking clock. Every hour the small clock would chime and announce the time.

Chapter 50

I had only been in Carstairs a few weeks when I started to hear horror stories from around the hospital. I heard talk of two patients who had escaped and murdered three people in the 70s. Now, these two have been mentioned in loads of different books so I won't bore any readers by going on about them plus I will never know what really happened, so I will just stick to the facts.

They both met in Carstairs where they were deemed insane. They had both murdered, were deemed untreatable psychopaths and were jailed for life without parole, which was a first for Scottish law.

They killed a nurse and a patient in one of the wards in Carstairs and then after getting over the fence they murdered a policeman on the outside. They were both apparently mentally ill but obviously their treatment in the State Hospital wasn't working. They were both jailed for natural life sentences. They were told that they would both die inside jail. One of them is now out and about, free on the streets. The other is still inside after a total of more than 40 years, but I can promise you that later in this book, he gets what's coming to him.

When the Carstairs killings happened 'X' was due to be released but 'Y' had other ideas. I don't think 'X' knew he was going to get out but if he had would that have stopped him (*or them*)? Maybe 'X' wouldn't have escaped on his own which will never be known.

Chapter 51

I got restrained a few different times mostly for raising my voice. One time one of the nurses who restrained me gave me medication. I was told to swallow it, or they would inject me. I'm scared of needles, so I had no choice but to swallow this liquid medicine. I was then held in a room until the haloperidol took effect. After 10 minutes it made me feel the most anxious I've ever felt in my whole life. It was like a bad trip. It was horrible. I was cracking right up and I was told to sit on the floor in a room.

When the ward manager came into Lomond Ward, she shouted at the staff who gave me this medication. She ordered me procyclidine to take away the horrible side effects. It worked and I came back around to my old normal self.

The next day I was told that I was not mentally ill. I had a personality disorder and I suffered a drug induced psychosis with paranoid thinking distortions. This led to bizarre behaviour in court. When I told the other guys in the ward I had a personality disorder, they told me I was very lucky to be going back to jail because there were men who had been kept in Carstairs for years with personality disorders. I was told that there was a man who had been in for over 30 years because he set fire to a pair of curtains in a hotel.

I heard that someone has to be at least 18 years old before they can be diagnosed with a personality disorder, but I was only 17 and got told I had one. The head doctor also told me that I would be going back to jail. I was delighted and was now expecting hopefully five years in a young offender's institution.

I was fully committed (*remanded for 110 days*) which meant that the police had 80 days to indict me. They came and indicted me before the 80 days ran out. I was indicted to appear at Greenock Sheriff Court and the charge had been reduced again to assault to severe injury, permanent disfigurement and permanent impairment.

When one of the other patients saw the indictment, he laughed and told me that I would get three years. Then my lawyer came and told me that I was going to the High Court for a tougher prison sentence. My lawyer told me the injuries were atrocious. The boy bled profusely and was moved from Inverclyde Royal Hospital to the Southern General in Glasgow. My lawyer also told me that he would need to get me a QC (*Queen's Council*) to act in my defence. When I was at the High Court, a QC would have to represent me.

When I moved into my flat in Greenock, I only lasted two months before I got myself arrested. I told the nurses in Carstairs that I drank every day and some of them told me that when they were 17, they drank every day too.

I was due to go back to court after my 12-week assessment but after 11 weeks I was moved to Kelvin Ward. The doctor told me that I was going back to jail, then the nurses moved me to the troublemakers ward a week before I was due to leave. I was appearing at court in one more week and I was sent to the Carstairs bad boys' ward.

I didn't misbehave in there as I was frightened they might keep me indefinitely. I did wind some of the patients up for something to do to pass the time, as I was bored. I was told to stop noising up the natives.

When I went to Kelvin the staff in the ward wound me up all week, constantly telling me that I would be coming back to Carstairs after court. On my first day in Kelvin the bullying from the staff started.

Meanwhile, there was a murder in my village. The Kilmacolm killer was a woman who strangled her own mother then stuffed a soft toy down her throat. This all happened in the retirement home around the corner from my house at the Cross. This kind of thing had never happened before. Murders didn't happen in Kilmacolm and after the woman was caught can you guess where she was locked up? (*Carstairs*) but I never saw her. I went back to prison. This was a big coincidence, two people from Kilmacolm being sent to Carstairs for violent crimes. Although we never met and just missed each other by a few weeks there was another coincidence. We were both assessed and deemed fit for prison and sent back to jail. After Carstairs the Kilmacolm killer only got four years. I was set to pay for my debt and I learned not to fret. But just how long was I going to get?

Chapter 52

I went back to Greenock prison. I was only back in jail a week and I was smoking hash again. The paranoia came back with a vengeance. I thought I was going to get done over in there.

I had to wait a few weeks until I went back to court and get sentenced. I was just so glad to be out of Carstairs. I didn't really like Gateside although after a few weeks I got used to it. I was just so happy to be back in the prison population.

The food wasn't as good and time dragged in. Long days, long weeks, but it never bothered me like Carstairs did. Not a place in Scotland could. Dykebar was terrible too and also my first ever night in Gateside. At least I was back in jail.

I was sharing a cell with a guy who got ecstasy, heroin and hash. So, I tried smoking heroin in Gateside prison in February 2003. We were what you call 'chasing the dragon' in our cell. Then I tried to get a bit of hash smuggled in at a visit, but we were caught in the visit room. My visitor Dave got arrested and got two years probation for the attempted smuggle. I was then put on closed visits. This meant that all my visits were through a glass screen.

A few weeks after getting back to Greenock jail, I met a boy, who was a year older than me and we liked each other so we asked the screws to put us in a cell together. I had been in three months and Andy was in doing a three-week remand and after this he got out. We wrote to each other and I would phone him from jail.

After Andy got out, I asked the screws to put me in with another boy I knew from the Gap Project and Unity Enterprise. So, Lee came into my cell with me.

On the end of February (2003) I pled guilty to assault to severe injury, permanent disfigurement and permanent impairment at Greenock Sheriff Court. The judge called for social enquiry reports and I was kept in Gateside for another three weeks until I was due back at court for sentencing, with my lawyer still telling me that I would be getting remitted to the High Court.

This was my first offence so that had to be taken into consideration. I would have been delighted with three years, but my lawyer and QC made it clear that I would be getting remitted to the High Court and would get five years.

My QC was fighting to keep my conviction at a sheriff court level. All I could hope for was the sheriff courts maximum prison term (three *years & 11 months*) with some sort of discount. This was my first offence which had to count.

Chapter 53

My mum and dad were both at court on the day of my sentencing. My QC was late getting to court, so I was recalled later that day. The judge gave my lawyer cheek because my QC wasn't there. When my QC arrived, I was taken back up the stairs into the court and the judge showed my QC sincere respect. This doesn't happen every day, in fact it is very rare for someone to appear at the sheriff court with a QC defending them.

QCs represent offenders when they are at the High Court but apparently, I was waiting to get remitted there for a longer sentence. My QC told me that other guys had been jailed for 12 years at the High Court for what I had done.

The Procurator Fiscal gave his speech making me out to be a brutal, mindless thug who had inflicted several serious wounds to an innocent victim. Then my QC told the court that what I'd done was barbaric. I was pleading guilty and this was my defence speech! I couldn't believe that my legal representative said this. My throat went dry and I thought that my QC, along with the PF, were trying to stitch me up. Halfway through my QC's babble the judge called for a break. I was taken back downstairs and put back into a court cell. I knew all QC's were Queen's Council and bound under Queen and Crown. I thought that my legal counsel along with the court law had sailed me up the river. A short time later I saw my legal team. I sacked my QC. He told me that he thought the judge was away to research a law remitting me to the High Court. I sacked him anyway.

He was bound under legislation to uphold the Queen's Law and I did not want this man of the Crown defending me at the High Court either. My QC went away with my lawyer, then two minutes later my lawyer returned and explained to me that this QC *(that he had got me)* was really good and that I was to trust my solicitor. I didn't have anything to lose now. I was told I was going to the High Court and I needed this QC. I decided to hold my head up high and let this QC throw me to the wolves and I took my lawyer's advice.

My QC never came back to see me. I was put back into the cell for a short time, then it was opened. I was handcuffed and marched back up to court for the third time on that day in regard to my indictment.

When court started my QC told the judge that I suffered a para-noid psychosis and had been diagnosed with a personality disor-der which made me believe my victim was going to take my house from me. He also told the judge that I had sacked him minutes before and then reinstated him because I was baffled.

The judge told my QC that he was going to deal with it. This made me so happy. I felt another big relief, like leaving Carstairs but now I felt excited. I was standing in the dock with butterflies of excitement. I now had no fears, I knew I was going to get roughly three years.

Chapter 54

I got 30 months. I was sentenced to two and a half years detention in a young offender's institution. And I was also given a full back dater, so the months I'd spent in Carstairs and then jail, came off my sentence. I only had 11 months left to serve. You automatically serve half your sentence as long as you are doing under four years. I would only have to serve 15 months out of my 30 months sentence. This was another great happy day of my jail life.

Going from being first told that I was getting jailed for seven or eight years and actually only getting sentenced to two and a half is incredible.

I was first charged with attempted murder on the Saturday, then on the Monday, I was jailed for danger of life. Then I was indicted for assault to severe injury, permanent disfigurement and permanent impairment.

Previously the police caught me with a pair of nunchucks. The Greenock Telegraph wrote that I was caught with Chinese fighting sticks but at court they were classed as Japanese fighting sticks.

My QC used the reports from the doctors at Carstairs which stated that at the time of the attack, I was suffering a psychosis which triggered a psychotic episode. The fact I had been sectioned in the State Mental Hospital helped the length of my sentence be cut shorter than normal circumstances. I never got remitted to the High Court.

I was taken back to jail over the moon. I was excited. I wasn't even nervous. I was buzzing. I would only have to do a year in the jail and then I would be out. I was told I was getting a big sentence and I got 30 months.

I was marked down as a YO (young offender) lodger and two days later I was taken by a Scottish Prison Service van to the young offender institute. After my time in Carstairs I only had to do a year in the jail. In Carstairs I couldn't stop thinking of getting out. I was wanting two things, to get out of Carstairs and to get out completely, but this wasn't going to happen in one go. As soon as I got my indictment my lawyer kept telling me that I was going to get five years at the High Court. I had a QC, that's how serious it was, but now I was delighted. I would be getting out in months, not years.

Chapter 55

HMYOI Polmont is an old borstal, near Falkirk, which was changed to a young offender's institution. It holds boys from 16 to 21, but I have been in the wing with boys at 14 and 15 because there was no room in any secure units. I heard of boys who were kept until they were 23. I was still only 17 so I was put in the under 18's unit in Lomond Hall (*west-wing*). It was March 2003 and I was put in the schoolboy's wing. It was Friday, then Monday came and I was opened up in the morning to go to induction. I went to two weeks induction which was a thing every YO (*young offender*) had to go to when they got sentenced. After induction was finished, I was given a job at IT (*computing*). This was my first work party.

I was on Lomond top flat which was for drug free schoolboys. Then I was drug tested and I failed for cannabinoids. I was down-graded and moved to the lower part of the hall on the bottom flat. There were more drugs on drug free top flat than there was on the drugged-up bottom flat. I know this because after a month I was given a job as a pass man and I was opened all day and my job was to clean the lower part of the hall. So, I knew where the drugs were and who had them. Whenever I smelled hash coming from someone's cell I would go to the boy's door and offer to get him opened and I'd ask him if we could smoke some of his hash.

I got some of the screws to open different cells and let them out for a shower or to use the phone and I would get some hash. Most boys don't really like being in their cells so when I offered to get them out that was a good offer. I loved being in my cell. That was my favourite time in jail, being locked in a cell for the night, the earlier the better.

Even when I was in Carstairs my favourite place was my room (*cell*) so that I could get away from the lunacy. In jail at the weekends you get locked up at teatime until the next morning and I loved my weekend dub ups. I know this will come across as outrageous because people aren't meant to like jail, but I can honestly say that I loved Polmont. I loved it that much I knew I would be coming back. I wanted to stab guys and I did think that I could do years in Polmont no bother. Because I knew I loved it. I kept all my newspaper cuttings and I wanted to be back in the newspapers again.

When I went back to Gateside I didn't enjoy it but Polmont was brilliant. After Carstairs I loved my so-called punishment. I thought violence and madness was all fun, I know I'm not the only one.

Chapter 56

After a few months in Polmont my gran died. She was my dad's mum and I love her very much. When we found out that she was dying of cancer I got to go and see her in the hospital. I was cuffed to a prison warden. I saw her for over an hour. It broke my heart seeing her like that, dying of cancer.

I also went handcuffed to a screw to her funeral. It was very sad. I took a cord and I helped lower her down into the grave. I wrote her a poem in my cell and the minister read it out. Then I threw the poem in my gran's grave and we buried her with it. That was the only time I was upset in Polmont, but my gran was a Christian and I know she is in heaven.

Paul who I knew from drinking in Bridge of Weir was in Glenochil Detention Centre. He was sentenced to 12 months for assault and robbery then the DC closed down and he came back to Polmont. I saw him a couple of times and then he got out. I never used to like him because he was angry when he was drunk. When I was in jail with him, I realised that I did quite like Paul.

After I turned 18, I got moved from the schoolboys' wing to Iona Hall bottom flat. I was put in a single cell again. I lost my job as the pass man because I was no longer in Lomond, so I didn't have a job.

A month later I was moved up to Iona 2nd flat and I went into a double cell. I asked for a single cell then a few hours later my cell door was opened and Andy walked in. We were to share a cell again but this time we never asked the screws, it was a coincidence. This was our other cell and this time we were both convicted serving prison sentences.

Andy battered a teenager with a plank of wood for shouting hurtful insults about his dead mother. He was sentenced to three years at the High Court in Glasgow.

This was our first sentences. We were both 18-year-old boys on the road to nowhere. We thought the jail was great and violence and madness was amazing.

We both went to Greenock Sheriff Court together. We weren't co-accused, we were appearing in court for different matters, but we went from our cell to the court together, handcuffed to each other in the police van and then put in the same cell in Greenock Court. We were literally inseparable. My court case was for possession of a pair of nunchucks. I was on good behaviour in jail. Andy was going to trial along with two other boys for a stabbing.

This was Andy's second trial. He walked on a 'not proven' verdict for assault to severe injury. He was cleared of hitting a man on the head with a piece of wood. On Andy's second trial, along with another two boys, they were charged with chasing a boy tripping him up and striking him on the body with a knife to his severe injury and permanent disfigurement. Andy was accused of tripping the boy who got stabbed. Another boy was charged with chasing him.

A boy I met in jail called Paddy, was charged for the stabbing but walked and so did the other boy who chased him, but Andy was found guilty of tripping the boy up. The judge sentenced him to serve another 11 months concurrently.

A boy who was charged with Andy, handed him hash at two different times in the dock during trial. I know this because I was sharing a cell with him and when he came back from court, we would get stoned every day and talk about his court case. On the last day of the trial we got stoned and laughed off the guilty verdict. At Christmas time Andy got some cocaine smuggled in and I tried it mid December 2003.

Then while we were at work the screws were prowling through our cell and found a tinfoil top for a bottle pipe and busted us for drug paraphernalia. I took the blame as Andy had over a year left, but I had under two months.

I failed a drugs test for hash and got moved to Argyll Hall (*north wing*). At this time Iona Hall was just newly built and housed all the drug free prisoners. North wing didn't have toilets in the cells it was porta potties and there was no sink to wash your hands either. It was disgusting but for some strange reason I still loved it.

I was getting out in a few weeks but beforehand I missed another Christmas. The first Christmas I was in I was in Carstairs, which broke me. But then I loved Polmont (*but not on this day*), it was miserable. I was actually ashamed of myself for being in jail on Christmas day. I should have been at home with my family.

I met another boy inside called Neil. He was doing four years for stabbing a man in Greenock. Then he battered a screw in Polmont and got another six months at the Falkirk Sheriff Court. He served three years and enjoyed his sentence the same as me and Andy did.

In later years when we were both grown men, me and Andy would phone each other and laugh and joke about our time in Polmont. We both agreed that HMYOI Polmont were the best days of our lives.

A part of me wished that I had got the original eight years for attempted murder. Or even six years for danger of life, but I only got two and a half years and I was very excited about getting out. Even though I thought Polmont was great, I couldn't wait to walk out the gate on my liberation date.

Chapter 57

I had quite a lot of what were supposed to be enemies in the jail, but I faced every single one of them and nothing happened to me. There were different boys saying that they were going to attack me in every hall in Polmont and when I faced them none of them did anything to me. I read a verse in the Bible (*what can mortal man do to me?*) and I made it my prayer and God kept me safe. I was a model prisoner and I would sit and eat my dinner with these boys who apparently wanted to knife me. I did feel a bit worried about all the jail gossips telling me that I was going to get attacked in every hall, but I also felt excited about facing them all.

On January 2004, a few weeks before I was due to be released I was taken back to court for a pair of Japanese fighting sticks but I got admonished which meant I didn't have to do any more time in jail. I was over the moon to be getting out in a few short weeks. I went in on October 2002 and I got out on February 2004. Which meant I was locked up for the whole of 2003.

When I got charged with attempted murder on the early hours of the Saturday morning my mum and dad prayed for the boy that I attacked and so also did members of their Church. Then on Monday the charge was dropped down to danger of life. This very rarely happens. When someone is up for attempted murder, if the charge gets reduced it normally takes months, but it happened over the weekend.

This all happened when I was 17 and I hope no one thinks that I'm being obscene. But I believe that God did intervene.

Chapter 58

I couldn't sleep the night before I got out. I was like a child on Christmas Eve. I got my freedom at about 7 o'clock on Monday 2nd February 2004. My mum and dad came and picked me up. I was standing in the grounds of Polmont waiting for the gate to open, when it did, I felt a very powerful experience of energy and excitement. I was buzzing, it was still dark, my mum was crying.

I was tired due to lack of sleep, but my excitement kept me awake. I was as excited as an 18-year-old boy could be. My mum and dad gave me a big cuddle and I was crying too, it was emotional. I should've just kept my head down and screwed the nut. My poor parents thought that my jail journey was over.

When I got sentenced to 30 months, I also got a 9-month supervised release order, so I had to go to the criminal justice team as soon as I got to Greenock. Then I went back home to Kilmacolm and went for a half bottle of Buckfast. When I finished it, I bought another half bottle and ended up drunk.

I then went to the Fox and the Hounds pub in Houston and had a few drinks. Then I went back and had a family dinner. It was a great day getting my freedom back. Then about nine o'clock that night I don't know what happened, but I burst out crying. It was awful. I cried myself to sleep. I wanted to go back to jail anyway and I wanted to stab boys to take me there. I was wanting to get myself a few years.

This was the only thing that gave me peace in my heart from this horrible feeling that I had, knowing that I was going to get myself the jail again for stabbing someone and I knew that I would get a girlfriend.

The next day I woke up and I felt great. I was out after a 30-month sentence and I was very cheerful. The following day, which was Wednesday, a man held a blade to a shopkeeper's throat in Kilmacolm and also robbed the corner shop of a sum of money. I got out on Monday and the newspaper shop got done on the Wednesday. Everyone was saying that it was me. They were saying that I had just come out of jail and that I had done it.

Another time I went up near Aberdeen for the weekend to my aunt's and the Co-op and the Victoria Wine shops (*which was on my street*) got robbed. Again, everyone in Kilmacolm said it was me that had robbed both shops. Even after the culprit died in jail, people still think that it was me. This time the robber used an imitation gun and robbed the place while he wore a mask (*covering his face*).

Chapter 59

I took a knife with me and I got the bus down to Greenock, back to Kenilworth looking for guys who I thought deserved to be stabbed. I just wanted to make a name for myself. I knew everyone was talking about me being in Carstairs but now I was out and wanted to be back in the newspapers again. Polmont didn't deter me I loved it.

Through my own choices and severe stupidity, just over five weeks after getting out I nearly got killed. I was hit on the head with bottles, bats, a machete and I was slashed and stabbed. I also had my head kicked in and stamped on. I nearly died but don't remember a single thing about it. It was a Friday night and my mum ran me to Greenock where I went up the stairs and sat in my ex-girlfriend's house in the same close, I used to live in. I drank a bottle of Buckfast and then I swallowed seven blue valium, before I finished my wine. I remember listening to music and I felt the valium hitting me and that is all that I can remember.

In an intoxicated manner I went looking for trouble and it didn't take long to find it. Within some minutes I was carved up and bashed to the ground. Luckily, I was wrecked and I can't remember anything about what happened to me.

The guy who sold me the valium was previously on the Trisha Show proclaiming that he had finished with drugs. If only he had.

I was brought up in Kilmacolm and Port Glasgow, but I was born in Greenock and then I lived there for a while in my teenage years. In Greenock I was left for dead. I was born and bled.

Chapter 60

I was in hospital for a week. I got a blood transfusion and 33 stitches, staples on my head and glue on my face. I'm terrified of needles and I had to get two new pints of blood through an IV drip. I remember waking up when a nurse was pulling the staples in my head out. It was horrible.

Andy phoned my dad from Polmont because he'd heard that I'd been murdered but obviously I hadn't. The Gap Project had heard that I had been killed as well. Patman was down in England hiding from the police and his dad phoned and told him that I was dead too.

As soon as the paramedics got me to hospital by an emergency ambulance, the doctors put me into an induced coma for two days. I was in intensive care. I later heard that a fire engine was sent out to hose my blood from the street. I also heard that a shopkeeper washed away some of my blood from the road as well. I was left for dead at the Kenilworth shop.

When I came out of the high dependency unit, I was put into the ward that my mum worked in. After a week in hospital, the CID came to see me. They told me that they had arrested three boys and charged them with attempted murder. I just ignored them and refused to speak. My dad told them that I wouldn't tell them anything. Then the CID blamed me of hitting one of the boys with a machete, on the same night that I had been almost murdered. I was getting accused of chopping one of the boys on the arm with a machete and also that I stabbed another one of the boys on the buttocks. I couldn't remember anything about getting nearly killed and here I was getting accused of knifing two of the three boys who had been charged with attempting to murder me.

The police must have thought that because there was an attempt made on my life that I would talk but I never. Then they blamed me of knifing two of the three boys. My head was in bits. I closed my eyes and told them nothing. One of the CID officers told me that if it was up to him, he would lock every one of us up in the jail for years for fighting in the streets. I was angry and frustrated that three boys were locked up in the police station because of me.

The other boy that got chopped collapsed on the street and was taken to the same hospital as me but in a different ambulance. He signed himself out the next day, then he was arrested a few days later and got charged with the attempted murder of me along with two other boys.

The nurses got a psychiatrist to come and see me because I was cracking up in my mum's ward. The doctor wanted to section me. He said I had post-traumatic stress disorder (PTSD). When I heard the word section, I thought of Carstairs. My limp turned into a march and I left the hospital. I couldn't even walk properly but I limped out of the IRH in Greenock. The nurses told me that I wasn't fit to be discharged and I needed another blood transfusion. I left anyway after only a week in hospital.

I wanted to be in the newspapers again and the attack on me was front page news in the Greenock Telegraph three times. It read *Teenager Slashed And Left For Dead*. Then when the boys were at court it was front page again, twice. It was a murder bid.

I can't remember anything about the attack on me but all I knew was that I'd brought this all upon myself. I got my wish, now everyone knew I was back out of jail, but it almost cost me my life, when I was cut to ribbons with a machete and a knife.

Chapter 61

After being nearly killed I was left a mess. All the wounds were to my head and I am left covered in scars. The hospital doctors told me another hit to the head might kill me. I was only 18 years old and I was butchered within an inch of my life. The attack on me did make me question my lifestyle but I was humiliated at what happened and this made me vow revenge. My head was fried, I felt physically and mentally weak, so I turned back to Buckfast and started drinking every day again. I was smoking hash again which I got addicted to almost instantly.

I had tried heroin when I was locked up and when I came back out people in my crowd were on it on the outside. So, I took smack with them too (*but not every day*). I had a rule which I gave myself, never two days in a row. But how long would this last?

On my 19th birthday after I opened all my presents my dad asked me if I got everything I wanted and I told my mum and dad that I did, but I was miserable. My mum told me that I looked terrible and that I should get off the drink and hash. I didn't get everything I wanted. I wanted to murder one of the boys who nearly killed me and it made me feel depressed. I wanted to go back to Polmont, but I only had two years left before I turned 21.

I began to read books on homicides and I watched the news most nights and very quickly I became obsessed with Scottish murders and I wanted to do one. I fantasised being on the news and I wanted to be in all the different countries newspapers. I was prepared to go to jail for years. I wanted to be a front-page killer. I thought that this would make me look even more notorious than I ever felt before. I wanted to get myself a lifer.

I had used knives before, but my victims had survived. Now I wanted to take it to the next level by stabbing someone to death. I created a false persona for myself. Really, I was just a young boy with a damaged ego. Deep down I was terrified, but I felt I had something to prove and that I had to show face. The thoughts that I had in my head along with the lifestyle I was living can only be described as total carnage. I wanted to be a psycho.

I went to Tenerife where there was a heat wave and the temperature fried my brain. I laid low in a bar with two gay guys unaware of their sexuality. I drank beer and Southern Comfort every day with Pernod.

I had just been awarded DLA *(disability living allowance)* two days before we flew out to Los Christianos. I got drunk every day and fantasised of revenge in the sweltering sun.

Then I came back and I teamed up with Neil who I had met in Polmont and I ended up in hospital for three days with a broken thumb and had to have two operations to save my most important right finger. When I came out the hospital, the police arrested me for attacking two men. The police were blaming me and Neil. I said, "No Comment" to every single question.

Two men had been knifed in my housing scheme and I was arrested. A 20-year-old man was slashed across the face and a 42-year-old man was cut up and stabbed on a Saturday night. I kept my mouth shut and an hour later I was back out. Neil didn't get out, he was recalled to jail for years because he was caught in a stolen car. He was out on prison licence and he didn't have a driver's licence! The CID drove a Ford Focus and they caught him in a stolen Ford Focus. He was locked up in jail for over three years for stealing one car *(bad Karma)*.

Chapter 62

Neil was in Gateside, so I visited him in there. Then he went to Polmont. I knew this visit room was easy. I had visited Andy in there a few times, so I smuggled hash into the Polmont visitor's room. I took a girl who would kiss Neil and give him valium from her mouth.

Andy got home leaves and on his second one he phoned and asked me to go down to his girlfriend's house for a drink. My dad ran me down and I bought Andy a bottle of wine. We drank and had a good night. I gave Andy his first bottle of Buckfast.

On one of Andy's other home leaves he was going back to Polmont on Monday and I was going to visit Neil on the same day at 2 o'clock. In my dad's car we drove Andy back through to the YO's. I never got into the visit. I was drunk, so I sat in the car with my dad. I wandered to a shop that I found to buy a half bottle of Buckfast.

Andy took drugs into Polmont for another boy and the girl who I took to give valium (*didn't just pass drugs*) she opened her mouth and told the boy what Andy was bringing in and Neil stole the drugs. I never even got into the visit room and people would have thought that it was all my fault because it was meant to be my visit. This girl tagged along and then told Neil about the parcel which he then stole.

Soon after this Neil got moved to Kilmarnock jail and I went to visit him in there. I never took him any hash the first time but the second time I took him in another quarter. I was visiting him faithfully until he asked me to stop bringing hash and instead take him other drugs. I did say that I would do it but then I never. I should never have taken hash in the first place and started it all up.

Neil apparently had ADHD, but he had never been diagnosed, although he displayed the symptoms. I had been certified as a boy who suffered every single symptom and I was to meet someone else who was the same as me. Only this person wasn't a boy.

I met a girl who also had ADHD. We had a one-night stand and took drugs together. I got some Indian food from the take-away then she fell asleep and I helped myself to her chicken korma. In the morning she wasn't happy. She pulled me out of bed and was screaming at me because I ate her korma while she was sleeping. I decided not to see her again, talk about bad karma, or was it bad korma?

Chapter 63

Andy got out of Polmont and phoned me on his release date. I went down to Greenock for a bottle. I had already drunk one and so had he and we got wrecked. It felt great both being free outside after our time in jail.

We went a walk to the shops in the west end of Greenock and then Andy ran after three boys, chasing them all up the road. Suddenly, I realised that he was chasing the boys who had been charged with attempted murder on me.

Round about this time the police came to my door serving me with a witness citation. I was summoned to court as a witness because I was the victim of a knife attack which nearly killed me. The three boys who were charged for the attack were pleading not guilty and were going to trial. I would not give evidence against them and I never spoke to the police in the hospital either so the boys must have known I wasn't informing on them. The charge for the attack on me had been reduced from attempted murder to assault to severe injury, permanent disfigurement and permanent impairment which was the same charge I got 30 months for.

When I got sentenced back in 2003 the maximum prison sentence at the Sheriff Court was three years, 11 months. Now the maximum term had been changed to five years custodial sentence at the Scottish Sheriff Courts.

The week before the trial was due to start the PF wanted to see me. When I walked into the Greenock Sheriff Court I was taken upstairs towards the fiscal's office. While we were walking up the stairs, I told the PF that the three boys who were charged never done it. I never even went into his office. I told him this on the stairwell, but he didn't believe me. He told me that the boys had signed statements, admitting they attacked me because I attacked them first. They were pleading self defence. I never saw any of their statements, but I knew the PF hadn't spoken to any of the boys either, so I told him that the police were lying. I told him that I knew it was his job to try and convince a jury that these boys were guilty. It was my responsibility to prove their innocence and that's exactly what I was going to do. So, the PF scoffed, shook his head and told me to leave, so I left.

I wanted vengeance but not rodent's revenge. I never got any of the boys back (*they got me back*). I think the lie I told the PF was quite smart because I made the whole court case fall apart, a week before the trial was ready to start.

Chapter 64

I got the case thrown out of court and there was talk that I was a rat because three boys got charged with attempted murder on me. There were also stories that they were in jail for attacking me. It's all lies.

I know a boy who got stabbed and slashed and he never had a criminal record, so he was pursuing a legal claim against his injuries. In the end the police were pestering him to name the boys who attacked him. He was to press charges in order to get compensation and the boys were to go to jail while he got his money.

The police told him if he didn't whistle his claim was over and he would not receive any payment for criminal injuries. He kept his mouth shut and he never got a penny, but at least Kal earned some honour.

I know most people would name their attackers for money and I don't know many people who would get three boys cleared of nearly killing them. I never named the boys, but even better I collapsed the entire criminal case.

I could've gone to court and told the truth that I couldn't remember a thing about the attack and maybe the boys would have still gone to jail but to me that is total humiliation. I put myself into this world and I didn't want to leave. I wanted my revenge.

I went back to drinking every day again. As soon as I opened my eyes I went for a bottle of wine. The shop opened just before eight every morning. Whenever I woke up, if it was any time after eight, I would get up, go and get a bottle of Buckfast.

One night I was drunk in my family home when my dad came into me and my brother's room and stated that I was an alcoholic. I just laughed because I thought my dad was joking but my brother agreed. At that moment it hit me, maybe I was.

I was 19 years old and I knew I was a drug addict plus I drank every day, but I didn't know if I was addicted to alcohol. I drank and took drugs daily which was a terrible link. After I was attacked, I did sink to the brink. It's like every time I would blink, I would think about drink.

Chapter 65

I wanted to kill one of the boys who nearly killed me, so I moved back to Greenock. I got a flat on Maple Road which I had for over a year. Then Green Oak Housing who owned the house were renovating all the flats, so I picked my new kitchen and bathroom. I used to stay in Greenock until my money ran out. Then I would go back to my family home in Kilmacolm, wait until I got paid and then go back to my flat in Greenock.

When the builders started working on my neighbour's flat, I knew that obviously my house would be next. My money ran out and I couldn't be bothered waiting on the builders. I gave my neighbour the key to my flat to give the workers, so that they could start their work while I went to Kilmacolm. Then I made my way back to my village.

At the same time that my neighbour's flat was getting done up, I was certain that I had killed her nephew. When I got home to Kilmacolm I checked the teletext expecting to read that there had been a murder in Greenock but there wasn't anything written.

That night I was hit on the head with a Buckfast bottle in Kilmacolm, so my mum ran me to the hospital in Paisley. She didn't want to take me to the hospital she worked in, for obvious reasons. After about an hour at Accident and Emergency I got fed up waiting so I stormed out. My mum reluctantly ran me back to Kilmacolm in her car where she put a bandage on my head.

We were parked outside my family home where we saw someone walking up the road wearing only one glove. It was a bit suspicious. It was two o'clock in the morning and he came walking up the street in pitch darkness wearing only one single glove. I knew the boy, so my mum ran him home to Port Glasgow where I stayed for the night.

He told me that he was up Kilmacolm breaking into cars. I told him that I had killed someone in Greenock and then had been hit with a bottle in Kilmacolm. That night the boy whose house I was staying at, decided to take his mum's car out for a spin. It wasn't her car; it was a courtesy vehicle. He drove us around Port Glasgow. We were jailbait because I sat in the front seat with a bandage on over my head and the boy didn't have a driver's licence.

The next day I went home to Kilmacolm where I bought a Greenock Telegraph in the afternoon, where I was sure that there had been a murder written in the newspaper *(that I'd committed)* but there wasn't. The only thing that was in the newspaper was that five cars had been broken into in Kilmacolm. Me and my mum knew who it was. The culprit was never caught but I stayed with him for the night.

There wasn't a murder at all in Greenock the boy survived. I tried to stab him through the heart but missed apparently by an inch. If the blade on the knife handle was a bigger size the boy would have died. I tried to take his life. I didn't care about the consequences. At this time in my life I wanted to get myself jailed for life. I glamorised notoriety.

If I hadn't tried to kill this boy, I would've found some other victim. I didn't even have any reason to kill him. I wanted to murder one of the boys who nearly killed me but never did. The only real reason I had was to make myself a murderer.

For a lot of people in Greenock violence is a way of life. And I left Kilmacolm because I wanted to live a violent lifestyle. I knew the boy's family would be in my house waiting on me, so I never went back to my flat. Out of paranoia I quit Greenock and I never became a murderer only an attempted murderer.

On that same night I started more trouble in Kilmacolm where there was further bloodshed. I got a Buckfast bottle smashed over my head and I'm now glad that the boy I tried to kill isn't dead.

Chapter 66

One morning my mum came in from working at the hospital and told me that a 20-year-old man had been murdered in Port Glasgow. The next day a boy from the Port came to my door to tell me who got killed. It was very, sad news. It was 'D'.

He was coming to Kilmacolm to camp for the night, but never made it. He stopped his taxi at the local petrol station and was then stabbed three times in the back. He drowned in his blood.

'D' was stabbed to death three miles from my house on the same street, only in the next town. He was coming to camp at the Knapp's, which is about half a mile from my house. 'D' stopped at the Burma Petrol Station and was killed as he got out his taxi.

'D' was coming to Kilmacolm, was killed on the Kilmacolm Road and was buried in the Kilmacolm cemetery. I attended his funeral and I saw and felt the heartache caused by his life being taken. I realised that I couldn't do this to someone's family. I was out to murder someone, but I realised I wasn't like one of these killers. I didn't want that anymore.

The boy who killed 'D' was an enemy of mine and he backstabbed me too, but not with a knife. He tried to hit me on the back of the head with a bit of wood, while I was fighting another boy. I turned around and grabbed the cosh before he had a chance to hit me with it, although, there were too many boys all hitting me at the one time, so I never had the chance to win the battle.

I was 20 and 'D's funeral was the first time I had ever been in a chapel (*Saint Francis of Assisi*). He lost his life before he could see 21. On the day that would have been his birthday, a group of his friends had a 21st heavenly birthday bash, up the graveyard. I will always remember the birthday present that I gave 'D' on his 18th. (*my happy birthday suit in court*).

His killer came out of jail that morning for possession of a knife and later that night stabbed 'D' to death with another knife. He then got jailed for life (*15 years minimum*).

Over the years I've been attacked by loads of different boys who ended up in jail for life for murder. Some people think I'm lucky to be alive but I've to thrive because God made me survive.

Chapter 67

I still carried a knife with me everywhere I went, but I no longer wanted to kill someone. Now I needed a blade on me because I had that many enemies (*or I thought I did*). I was certain that I was determined to murder one of the boys who nearly killed me, so I carried a knife with me everywhere I went. Twice when I never had a knife on me, I saw one of the boys who attacked me. Two days in a row I saw the same boy. This made me feel even more determined to carry a knife and to use it for violent vengeance.

Around about this time I was constantly being arrested and interviewed for knife attacks. A 20-year-old man told the police that I slashed his face. Another 20-year-old man told the police I hit him on the head with a machete. I was arrested while wearing a stooky (*after my thumb was broken by a machete*). This guy was pressing charges against me, telling the CID that I chopped him but that's not all that he was saying. He stabbed the bin man in Greenock and blamed his two co-accused and got them eight years in jail. I met these two boys in Polmont and after my release while they were still doing LTP sentences, this informer was saying that I fractured his skull by hitting him with a machete. I normally said, "No Comment" but the CID told me that if I said that this time I would be getting charged. So, I did what anyone would do, I talked my way out of the situation.

I was arrested and accused of another attempted murder. A 23-year-old man told police that I stabbed him in the stomach a day before his birthday and also six days before Christmas. On the day after this attack, it was reported in the local newspaper which was the day of his birthday. He was kept in hospital until after the new year and when the CID spoke to him, he blamed me. This wasn't all that this guy was saying either. He jailed Paddy's brother for five years after he informed on him for chopping him with a machete. Now, he was telling the police that I nearly killed him. I was interviewed for slashing a policeman's son as well but wasn't charged for any of these attacks.

When I came out of Polmont I was on a supervised release order for nine months and I was accused of knife attacks left, right and centre, but never got charged for a single one. In the end up, I got a good report for my supervised release order. I think the supervision officer felt sorry for me because I was nearly killed myself.

My right thumb was broken by a machete and I was supposed to wear a stooky on my hand for a number of weeks but after a fortnight I cut it off with a knife in the bath. I was supposed to go to physio as well but never went to that either.

I lived my life back and forth going from Kilmacolm to Greenock. I would drink in Port Glasgow as well and I was tempted to get my old flat in Hole Farm Road back. I realised I didn't want to live in the bottom flat again because of the paranoia I felt before. Then a girl moved into it instead. When she wasn't in, someone kicked her front door in leaving it unlocked. I then went in and sat by myself. I missed the old place.

Kilmacolm has been declared the millionaire capital of Scotland. Greenock has the highest murder rate in the UK and Glasgow was the murder capital of western Europe. All three of these places are in the West of Scotland which is in western Europe. I wanted to get myself a stab proof vest because in Greenock stabbings were seen as the best and I was more or less living in the wild west.

Chapter 68

I started taking my mum and dad's cars out for joy rides. I drove from Kilmacolm to my flat in Greenock until one time I was caught and arrested. I got bail but had to appear at court for taking a car without the owner's permission and driving without a licence.

When I appeared at court, I got fined £100 and had three points put on my licence, which I never even had! I was in the Greenock Telegraph newspaper.

Later that week I went to a house in Greenock to buy some crack-cocaine. It was letterbox treatment. The dealer never opened the door. He served customers through the letterbox. When I told the dealer who I was, suddenly the door opened and I was invited in. Everyone else was told to stand and wait through the letter box, but I was given preferential treatment and taken inside.

Andy was in the flat with two men and one of them told me he had seen me in the newspaper and now he knew that I could drive. The other man was on his knees picking up bits of crack-cocaine off the floor and putting it into a pipe.

The man who was in charge asked me if I would do him a favour and drive a car through the chemist window at the bottom end of Larkfield. I told the man that I wouldn't, but he put pressure on me and I told him I would think about it. I left the flat then went back to my flat in Greenock.

At 10 o'clock my phone rang showing me Andy's mobile number, but I never answered it. Then it rang again, this time from a with-held number, but I ignored both calls.

Within a week I was arrested again for driving and I was taken to Greenock court the next day. On my night in the police station the turn-key put a Greenock Telegraph through my cell door. I looked through it and saw that Andy was in jail charged with attempted murder.

The next day I was taken to Greenock Sheriff Court and put in a cell to wait until my court appearance. Before I was due to appear, the cell door opened and Wilky walked in. I went up to court and was released on bail, but Wilky was fully committed. He was in for attempted murder too.

A few days later I went to see Wilky in Gateside and Andy was sitting in the same visit room. His girlfriend was visiting him. Later I phoned Andy's partner to arrange a visit so I could go and see him, but not intrude on any of her visits. She told me that he was out and asked if I wanted to speak to him and I did.

Andy had got out on a PF's release. I went back to visit Wilky a few weeks later and he told me that Andy was back in. Andy had been caught with a gun. I went and visited him and Wilky in Gateside at different times.

Then there was more trouble in Greenock. The man who asked me to drive a car through the chemist window and got Andy to stab a man, gave a shotgun to another man and on his orders, he shot two brothers in Larkfield. One of the brothers had been killed outright and the other brother was left disabled. Andy was supposed to shoot these two brothers and was given a shotgun with bullets but never did it. About a week later Andy was caught with the gun.

The two men who were charged with the shootings went on trial and the man who pulled the trigger got jailed for 25 years to life. The man who asked me to drive a car through the chemist was jailed for over 10 years for drug dealing. The two men who stood in the dock both had the same surname but were of no relation. One of the men standing, had only one leg and the other had only one eye. The leader wanted someone to drive a car through the chemist (*so he asked me*) because none of them would have passed a MOT!

Chapter 69

Looking back, I can't believe that I managed to stay out of jail for so long, but I was out for nearly two years and I carried a knife basically everywhere I went for over a year. I was in and out of the police station constantly getting interviewed for attacks, but they never had any evidence. I was eventually jailed for a breach of the peace. I refused bail, I wanted to go to jail. Now I was in Gateside with Andy and Wilky. I had been visiting them there since they got remanded, now I was in too. I never shared a cell with Andy this time, but I was next door to him and would talk through the pipe.

I rarely go to outside exercise when I'm in jail. I prefer doing my time in my cell but in Gateside I went sometimes. One day at exercise Andy was slashed across the face. I wasn't there, but the guy who slashed Andy had it in his head that I stabbed him, so I was lucky he never attacked me as well at any other time.

When I went to jail, I met loads of boys that I already knew from Kibble and I came across Eggy in Gateside. After three weeks, I went back to Paisley Sheriff Court where I pled guilty, but I never got a prison sentence. I was bailed for social enquiry reports.

On my way to court, Andy was in the same van as me. He was going to Glasgow High Court to plead guilty to possession of a shotgun. The reliance van dropped me off at Paisley and took Andy to Glasgow. I wished him all the best as I knew he would need it. I was at court for two breach of the peace charges and was sentenced to a £200 fine for each charge (*totalling £400*). I refused to pay the fine and told the judge that I wanted to take the days in jail, He denied me a prison sentence. I was told to leave the court.

Andy was given another three weeks on remand for social inquiry reports and was taken back to Gateside to wait to see how many years he would get.

I went to the Community Justice Office where I told the social worker that I wanted to go back to jail. The worker said that I was the first person she had ever seen that actually wanted to be jailed. I was a bit surprised because I loved being in Polmont.

I was in the front page of the Paisley newspaper. They called me a lout who was refused the jail. Andy was jailed for six years and was moved to the hall in Gateside which held long term prisoners, but then he got caught with a banned mobile phone and was moved to Glenochil Prison. Wilky went to Carstairs.

Since I was a teenager I would drink and take drugs with a police officer's son. People said that I corrupted him. Although 'M' loved the drink and drugs that he took, but they fried his brain. He lived in the houses right next to the Kilmacolm police station with his parents, but he lost his marbles. Along with the drugs he took and beatings that he ended up taking, he went behind his door and never showed his face for years. He went totally paranoid.

Very many years ago Kilmacolm was apparently called Kilmalcolm and the poor boy didn't come out his house in Kilmacolm for years because he thought that people wanted to kil-malcolm!

Basically, the only time he would come out his house was to go to the shops to buy his alcohol. When I got sober, I noticed that he drank every day, but when I questioned him about it, he denied having a problem.

I call him 'M' malcontent because he doesn't have much of a life and he rebelled against his father who was a policeman. Drink and drugs were his life, but now he doesn't have much of an existence. The drugs he took fried his head (*as they did mine*). He drinks every day on his own to make himself feel fine. Now all he has left, is his wine.

Chapter 70

One day I was looking for money in my family home. I wanted a drink but had no cash so in my search I ended up in my mum's room where I found a bank card. It was a Celtic Master Card and I had previously found the pin number as well.

Acting on impulse I took the bank card and went on a spending spree. I bought wine and hash, but I partied on regardless.

About a week later (*the day before my wee sister's birthday*) I bought the Greenock Telegraph and I noticed that there was a column on puppies for sale and it was my favourite dog. A Staffordshire Bull Terrier.

Acting on impulse (*again*) I phoned up the woman and asked her if I could buy one of the staffy pups and she told me there was only one left for sale. I phoned my mum and dad and told them that I had been given a dog for free. The next day, my sister's birthday, I went and bought the puppy for £150. I got a taxi from Maple Road to Finch Road in Greenock, via the cash line, where I bought the staffy bitch. I took the dog in the cab and the taxi driver told me that staffies are very bad chewers, so I would need a cage as well, to stop the animal chewing my mum's house. I had two girls with me and one of them had her nephew with her. I dropped them off at my flat with the puppy, then I got the taxi down to a pet shop in Greenock so that I could buy a cage, which I paid £50 for. I bought dog food for puppies and then out of guilt I cut the bank card up with a pair of scissors.

I had full intentions of breeding the dog, but my dad got her neutered when I was back in jail because she had a phantom pregnancy. The vet warned that if bred, she could develop cancer so out of worry my dad got her spayed.

That day I bought the puppy, I took her back to Kilmacolm for my wee sister's 11th birthday and she was over the moon. She called her Kizzy. The next day I was 20 years old.

This was what I did on my last day as a teenager. I bought a dog for my sister with my mum's stolen credit card. My mum worked as a nurse and she had to hide her purse because temptation is a curse.

Chapter 71

I was due to attend court for assaulting a window cleaner, but I never appeared. A warrant was put out for my arrest and in May (2005) the police came and lifted me out of my house in Kilmacolm. I hid in the cupboard in my bedroom as soon as I heard the police knock. Then my arresting officers walked right in and lifted me from my bedroom cupboard. One of the police officers said upsetting, offensive comments about my family and bullied me verbally on the road to the cop shop. When I got to the Greenock Police Station the arresting officers lied and told their duty officer that they caught me out on the street, as I was coming out my house.

I was held in the cells until court the next day, when I was remanded again for another three weeks. The police that arrested me charged my dad with perverting the course of justice because he never opened the front door of our house. My dad was in the living room working on his laptop, but the police charged him after bad mouthing him to me. My mum wrote a letter to the procurator fiscal and this case was thrown out of court. The charge was not entertained.

The next day some other police officers arrested my older sister and my younger brother at the Kilmacolm Fayre. My brother had just passed his driving test and was out drinking with friends. My sister was charged with trying to free a prisoner and my brother was charged with a breach of the peace. The police said that my brother was shouting and swearing at them and he had to be detained. Then my sister tried to free my brother but was arrested. So, when it went to court the judge found my brother 'Not Proven'. My mum wrote a letter getting charges against my sister dropped but my brother had to appear at court. He went to trial.

The judge couldn't find him not guilty because he wouldn't go against the police, but they lied at my brother's trial! The judge even said himself that he was not happy with the way the police had done their jobs.

I was in jail at this time and I was brought to court on the same day for unpaid fines. I was held in the cells under the court and my mum and dad were going from courtroom to courtroom. At this time my sister was applying to get into the police service and she worked in a children's unit. This charge made it impossible for my sister to join the police force and it could've damaged her career as well.

My big sister (*Natalie*) got promoted and worked in the locked units and after more promotions became manager of one of the secure units. The charge was thrown out and she was never found guilty of trying to free a prisoner, but never ever got into the police department. She was sabotaged.

My wee sister (*Bethany*) was sitting a final driving lesson before her driving test and for no reason the police pulled her over, which put her under pressure and she said she failed her driving test because of them. The driving instructor later told me that my sister was the only person who had ever got pulled over in his car.

A policeman used to follow my dad up the road, driving behind him growling with the diesel engine growling too. He terrorised my younger brother when he was school age. My mum reported him and he was kicked off the Kilmacolm run and sent to work at the Glasgow airport. The police have picked on my whole family except my mum who has written letters all the way to fight them.

I have been accused of slashing a policeman's son and another policeman moved downstairs from my family home underneath us. I stole a police cadet's car and wrote it off. It wasn't a police car; it was his own Corsa.

Because of my bad behaviour, my whole family has been picked on by officers of the law (*which was my lifestyle flaw*).

Chapter 72

My brother went for a drink with his friends and ended up hospitalised for the night. I am not giving glory to the boys who attacked him and if it appears that way, then there is no honour without vengeance.

I went over to Houston in my dad's car to help my brother. As soon as we pulled up at the Gryffe High School I could see my little brother lying on the pavement in a pool of blood. The boy who phoned me had his head smashed open and another boy got his cheek bone broken. My brother and one of his friends were kept in a hospital ward that night and so was someone else. Benny and Hammy got out of hospital the next day but the other boy was kept in for longer with his face smashed in.

I saw five ambulances that night and there were injured boys in them all. The Paisley newspaper wrote that two gangs were fighting and that there were four serious assaults and one attempted murder.

The police went into my brother's hospital room while he was in bed to interview him. My brother never knew what was happening. He couldn't remember a thing. This is a trick the police often use, as they did once with me.

Me and my brother can't remember a thing about our attacks. It is a loss of time for us both. Alcoholics call it a blackout. Although we were both in hospital at different times the coincidence is that the attack on me was attempted murder and I was getting interviewed for serious assaults. My brother's and Hammy's attacks were serious assaults and they got interviewed for an attempted murder (*extremely coincidental*) and when I found my brother hurt, I went mental.

Chapter 73

On Friday 13th 2005 I went to court for a trial. I am not superstitious, but I thought I would get jailed. I was up at court for assaulting a window cleaner and putting panic and alarm through another four window cleaners. They were all denying informing on me, so I wanted to go to trial but three of the window cleaners turned up at court to give evidence against me and following instructions from my lawyer, I pled guilty before the trial even started.

I expected to get jailed, but the judge bailed me and I was very surprised. When I went to walk out of court the police arrested me for failing to pay a fine for joyriding without a driver's licence. So, I was right all along and on Friday 13th I got locked up. After a weekend in the cells I was taken to court on Monday, when I was bailed and given extra time to pay my fine which I never paid.

When I was locked up underneath the court, Wilky was in one of the other cells. He was kept apart from everyone else because he was a mental patient at the State Hospital. The Carstairs staff who went with him to court, remembered me and thought that I had got myself the jail on purpose to pass him drugs because I was a former patient. They thought that I had orchestrated a drug manoeuvre. We were both annoyed, because we thought it was the patients that were supposed to be paranoid!

Chapter 74

I took my mum's car out for a spin and headed over towards Houston. When I was driving through Bridge of Weir, I saw the window cleaners. The window cleaner, who I was due at court for assaulting, pulled his mobile phone from his pocket and I knew he was phoning the police. I drove to Houston and turned at the roundabout at Saint Fillan's and headed back towards Bridge of Weir. When I drove by the kiosk shop the window cleaners were gone but when I turned at the corner the police were waiting for me at Bull's garage. They flashed me to stop but I kept on driving.

I was chased by the police back to Kilmacolm. I was up at the car's full speed (90mph) which was as fast as the Vauxhall Corsa would go. I managed to get away from the police, but I skidded round a corner and crashed into a garden fence. I got out the car and ran for it. As soon as I got into a field, I heard the police helicopter was out. I ran across the cycle track into Duchal Woods where I found a fox's den, which I hid in. I could hear the helicopter flying all over me. Then I heard dogs barking. I panicked automatically thinking it was the police dogs, so I got out and ran for it.

I could see the helicopter circulating the area looking for me. I hid under a hedge and waited for the pigs to fly away then I ran into another field. I could see the helicopter coming back so I hid again and again until I got away. I was going to jail anyway for a string of charges.

I managed to evade capture, but two days later two policemen walked right into my house and arrested me. I punched one of the policemen on the face and then I spat on the other officer's head. When I got to the charge bar at the police station, they put a paper mask on my face so that I couldn't spit or bite them.

The next day I was taken to court where I was definitely expecting to get jailed, but my lawyer done wonders and got me out for psychiatric reports and all my cases called together in two weeks' time. My lawyer told the judge that I had a personality disorder and the sheriff said it was obvious I had some kind of disorder. I had no respect for law and order.

The judge told me that I was going to get a lengthy sentence in jail but gave me bail. Whatever was wrong with me made it impossible for me to behave and the police called me the Kilmacolm crime wave.

Chapter 75

I got a taxi to Johnstone Job Centre to collect a crisis loan. I was given a giro of £20 and the taxi was £11 so I ran away with the driver chasing me. As I ran, a boy was watching from his window and he invited me into his house to hide. I went in and hid for a while with Yogi.

The taxi driver who gave me hard man stories, got the police to me. After all his football hooligan talk, he got the police onto me for bumping his taxi. The boy I met, Yogi, would phone and I would go through to his house in Johnstone, where we drank and took drugs.

On the 12th of July 2005 I went through to Johnstone to see Yogi but I couldn't find him at his flat in Cartside. I walked through the town and there was an orange walk taking place in the Johnstone Square, so I walked up to the train station with the parade.

When we all got to the Johnstone train station, I waited there for the bus to take me back home to Kilmacolm. Before the bus came, there was a commotion and a drunk woman fell onto the railway line. I was on the bus and didn't know what had happened. All the buses stopped and everyone was interviewed by the police.

I had a warrant out for my arrest for failing to appear at court so when the police asked me my name, I gave my brother's name and details. I told the police that I didn't see anything, which I hadn't. Eventually the police let the bus I was on go. When I came home, I told my mum what happened and she checked the teletext and the news report read that the woman had lost an arm and a leg.

A few weeks later the police phoned my family home to speak to my brother on my behalf telling us that they weren't taking it any further. This was the only time in my life that I have ever signed a statement. I was kidding on I was my brother and it was also the first ever time I had been involved in an orange walk. It's enough to put some people off.

Obviously, the drunken woman who fell onto the railway line won't be going on anymore orange walks, unless she's in a wheelchair. That's what can happen when you get intoxicated (*beware*).

Chapter 76

The police caught up with me and I was arrested again. My family went on holiday to France, so none of my family were at court for me in the gallery.

My lawyer told me that I would get 18 months, but I was praying that I wouldn't get that long. I got 16 months. The judge jailed me for three months for punching a window cleaner on the head and body, a further three months for punching a policeman on the face, five months for spitting on the policeman's head and another five months for the helicopter chase. I was also banned driving for two years.

Before I got sentenced, I did three remands. When I was in jail, I was 20, nearly turning 21 but I lied and told the screws in Gateside that I was only 19. They believed me and changed my DOB making me a year younger. I did this so that I could go back to the place I loved (*Polmont*).

On my third remand I got bail on my 21st birthday. I went to court from Gateside and the reliance sang happy birthday to me while I was put into the court cells. There was a screw in Gateside whose daughter visited me in the local jail, until her dad stopped her visiting. She still came and visited me in Polmont even after her dad pulled the plug on her in Greenock. I served another seven months in Polmont. I was loving it.

The Greenock Telegraph wrote that I committed a crime spree. Really it was a window cleaner spree. That's why I got that sentence because a certain window cleaner phoned the police on me on numerous occasions. He also told the police that I had been chasing him with a knife on different occasions.

This window cleaner thinks that he's a big hardman but deep down he is a coward. He uses the police to protect him and has been an informer for years and years.

His nickname is Biscuit and I have no idea why, but maybe it's because he crumbles and phoned the police, jailing me for assault (*and a breach of the peace*).

Chapter 77

I was back in Polmont and I was so happy. I was put in North Wing for three weeks and I was working in the packing work party. Then they moved me over to Nevis Hall which became the drug free hall at this time.

I was over the moon to be back in Polmont but a week later my bubble was burst. I was moved to Barlinnie. I felt my plan backfired four weeks later and I was gutted. The screws thought I was only 20 but they still shipped me out to the con's jail. There was about 10 of us YO's *(except me)* getting moved and we were all gutted. When we arrived at Barlinnie, a female screw said, *"Welcome to Hell"*.

I was put in the induction centre for the night, then moved over to A-Hall the next day. I was down as a non-smoker, so I was put into a cell with an old man about 60. I had over six months of this to face.

I was in A-Hall for a week, then I got moved over to D-Hall to the psychiatric unit for six months. After a couple of months, I realised that I quite liked Barlinnie.

In Polmont there were boys slashed and stabbed every now and then but not that often. I only ever saw one boy stab another with a pen, then he hit his attacker back with a kettle lead.

In Barlinnie, 2006, there was a slashing near enough every day, but I never saw a single one. HMP Barlinnie is probably the most infamous jail in Scotland. It's one of the most notorious institutions in Europe as well. They used to hang prisoners. I have seen the condemned cell in D-Hall.

One day I got a letter from a boy called Blaney who was in Friarton Prison in Perth. I wasn't expecting this letter, but I wrote back. I wrote to Paul as well.

Paul and Blaney drank together in Bridge of Weir. They were both in Gateside sharing a cell then they were both out together drinking again. I used to smoke hash and drink wine with Paul and I was in Gryffe High School with him and then Polmont.

Paul and Blaney didn't finish their sentences. They both got out on early release on the tag. Paul cut Blaney's tag off and he was taken back to jail to finish his sentence for breach of tag curfew. Paul breached his tag too.

I quite liked Barlinnie, but I missed another Christmas and felt the shame again. I was glad when the festive time was all over. I was due out in March but still had a string of outstanding charges to go to court for. I was doing 16 months, but my lawyer told me that I would get longer. I kept on praying that I wouldn't get any more time. I was praying that my sentence would stay at 16 months.

I went back to Paisley Sheriff Court for dangerous driving and was disqualified for another 30 months. I was given seven months to run concurrently which meant I didn't have to serve any more time in jail. This ran in with my 16-month sentence.

I went back to Paisley court again this time for assault. I punched a guy on the face. The judge sentenced me to six months concurrent. This meant that I didn't have to serve any longer. I then went back to the Greenock court for spitting on a window cleaner and I was jailed for two months to serve consecutive. This put my sentence up to 18 months and meant that I would have to serve a month extra (*Or did it?*).

My mum and dad's old Pastor came to see me at a chaplaincy visit within the prison and we both prayed that I wouldn't have to do the extra time. My prayer the whole time was that I wouldn't get 18 months, then when I eventually did, my sentence never changed and I prayed that I would only have to do my 16-month sentence.

I promised myself and my family that I wouldn't drink every day again, but my parents were convinced that I was an alcoholic. I still wasn't 100% sure if I was or not. The drink turned me into a lout, and I was in doubt, but I still planned on drinking the day I got out.

Chapter 78

The 6th of March came and I was facing another month in jail, when my prayers were answered. I got out. I served 8 months and didn't have to do the other month. The jail never put the time onto my sentence, so I got out a month early. My original prayer that I wouldn't get 18 months came true. When my lawyer told me,

I would get 18 months I prayed I wouldn't (*then I got 16*).

My prayer the whole time was that I wouldn't get any longer and that I would only have to do 16 months. Then when I got two months consecutive, (*just 2 weeks before I was getting out*) my sentence was supposed to go up to 18 months, but my liberation date never changed and I got out early.

Before I went back in, I was drunk every day which made me miserable. I didn't really like my life outside, but my plans were to live a happy life this time. I drank the day I got out. When I went to the shops to get my wine the CCTV camera followed me around the Cross. The police put the camera at the Kilmacolm Cross and it would follow me from the shops all the way up the road to my family home.

Within a month it caught up with me and I was drinking every day again. I was 21 and realised that I was an alcoholic. I turned 22, was drunk every day and I was addicted to hash again. I became depressed again and wanted to go back to jail so that I could get sober and come back out and try again.

I was living a life that was a drunken daze, I just couldn't achieve sobriety, which gave me severe anxiety. There was no way I could fit in to normal society.

Chapter 79

There was a big commotion on my girlfriend's street in Houston. Two Muslim suicide bombers tried to drive a car through the main entrance of the Glasgow airport. One of the terrorists set himself on fire killing himself, while trying to ram the car through the airport's doors and the other 'would be' suicide bomber, got out of the car and was (*no doubt*) planning on blowing himself up but he got put to the ground and jailed for his antics.

The two suicide bombers stayed on my girlfriend's street and they were both doctors for the NHS. One of them worked in the same hospital as my mum (*Inverclyde Royal Hospital*). I stayed over there on numerous occasions, on the same street which these terrorists lived on. We drove over in my mum's car and saw that the whole street was cordoned off.

One of these men was the doctor in the same ward my mum worked in, for six months and then he moved to Royal Alexandria Hospital in Paisley. After the terrorist attack at the airport the police removed the hospital computer in the ward my mum worked in.

They were two doctor bombers determined to kill themselves for their crazed religion. Two intelligent men brainwashed into planning out their own deaths for a cause. I believe God is loving and don't understand why anyone would think he wanted terrorism.

My two sisters went on holiday to different places at different times. Natalie went to Turkey and Bethany went to Thailand and on both their trips there was terrorist attacks. A few bombs went off in Thailand blowing up some of the street and killing people and in Turkey someone tried to shoot the president.

My girlfriend was overweight and promiscuous. She wasn't very nice and got passed about like a dice. I call her pizza because everyone gets a slice.

Chapter 80

When I was in jail one of my brother's friends was in a terrible accident. He crashed his car and was very nearly killed. He lost a kidney, was in a coma, had to learn to walk and talk again and was left simple.

Before this happened to him, he was a bit game. He left Greenock and came to Kilmacolm to make a name for himself and he nearly got one. He used to fight quite often and was caught with three different offensive weapons at different times.

I was with him when he got caught with a hammer and another time he was caught with a knife in Greenock. Finally, he was caught with half a pool cue as well. He was on his way to jail, but then was nearly killed when he wrote his car off.

He even thought that he could escape jail by joining the Army and went to sign up and so did I. Our paths crossed at the Greenock Army depot. We met each other outside and we walked in together. He told the recruiting Army Officers that he was up at court and was facing jail, so they sent him away until after the court outcome. Then he crashed his car and played the sympathy card and never went to prison.

I was told that I was banned from the Army for five years because I'd been to jail, so I was sent away too. Then we both went up to my flat in Greenock.

When he crashed, the speaker in his car smashed him on the back of the head and he will never be the same again, but even though he was left well retarded he will always be well regarded.

Chapter 81

Wilky phoned me from Gateside letting me know that he had been moved from Carstairs back to jail. He asked me to go and see him. About a week later I phoned up Gateside to book a visit when they told me Wilky had been moved to another jail. A short time later Wilky phoned again, telling me that this time he was in Barlinnie and still wanted to arrange a visit.

In Barlinnie, convicted prisoners book their own visits so I told Wilky to book a visit any day and he said he would get it organised. Before he hung up the phone, I asked him what hall, flat and cell he was in and he told me.

I was out on bail and was going back to jail. I was due up at Greenock Sheriff Court which meant I would end up in Gateside which was the prison I didn't like, but I never appeared at court and a warrant was put out for my arrest. Two days later I went up to Glasgow and threw a bottle of Buckfast at police officers. I was making my own way in to see Wilky.

I was handcuffed and taken to the police station in Stewart Street. I went to the Glasgow District Court the next day which was a Monday. Everyone else in the court cell was hoping to get out, but I wasn't. I didn't want bail. I wanted to go to jail to see Wilky.

A lawyer came to see me and told me that I would probably get out as I hadn't committed a serious offence and that they knew I had mental health issues. I would possibly get a fine. I sacked the lawyer and represented myself. I stood up in court and threatened the judge that if I didn't get jailed, I would go back out and get myself jailed again that night. So, I was given four months in jail.

All the other guys in the cell thought that I was mad. They couldn't understand why anyone would want to go to jail if there was a chance they could get out. I had my head set on going back in to keep Wilky company.

I missed the jail and I was drinking every day. I had been out for 10 months and my life was a misery. Before I got arrested, I prayed to God that I would get to share a cell with Wilky. I was taken to Barlinnie and I asked the officers to send me to B-Hall where Wilky was. I was put on the bottom flat of this hall. I was sharing a cell with a guy for two days, then he got moved to another prison. I was praying the whole time, that the screws would put Wilky and me in the same cell.

I was opened up for dinner and I asked one of the prison warders if me and Wilky could cell share. I told the screw where Wilky's cell was and the screw I approached was the B-Hall manager and he told me to go up the stairs and get Wilky and bring him back with me so that we could be together. I walked up all the stairs to the top flat and opened Wilky's spy hole. I looked in and saw him looking back at me. I declared myself whilst we both laughed away at the circumstances and while I told him to pack his stuff as he was coming into my cell with me. My outside prayer that had become an inside prayer was answered.

A few days later a visit confirmation slip came through our cell door which said that our visit was approved. We got a good laugh with us both sitting there locked up together in our cell, with this visit confirmation slip telling Wilky that a visit had been granted for me to come and see him. The visit would've lasted under an hour, but I was there for the duration.

The day before I went back to jail, I was walking about Glasgow City Centre looking for a way to get arrested. I found two policemen working the beat and I threw my Buckfast bottle at their feet on Sauchiehall Street.

Chapter 82

There is a rumour, or myth, that every cell has a Bible in it but believe me this isn't true. I asked one of the screws for a Bible and he told me that there wasn't even one in the whole hall. He then asked me what religion I was (*Catholic or Protestant*) and I told him that I was a Protestant. The screw then got a Minister to come and see me.

When the Reverend came to see me, he asked me why I wanted to see him. So, I asked him for a Bible. Within an hour I was given a brand-new copy of the good book. I didn't read it. I put it up on a shelf above the television. A couple of days later I was sitting at the desk below the TV when suddenly the Bible fell onto the desktop. The Bible had opened itself up and I looked down and started reading it. Wilky who was sitting in his bed watching what had just happened, asked me if I always read the Bible wherever it opened. I told him that this was the first time this had ever happened.

I began to read from corner to corner and what I read was the parable of the prodigal son. While I was reading this, I could feel the Power of God coming all over me and this parable touched my heart and meant something to me. At this time, I didn't know what, but then my families old Pastor came to see me at a pastoral visit in the chaplaincy. I told him what happened with me reading the prodigal son and how it meant something to me, but I didn't know what. The pastor then told me that his wife had done teachings on this parable a week or two before and in the last week, five different people, had told them that the parable of the prodigal son had affected their lives. I asked him if that meant that I was the sixth person and he told me I definitely was and I believe this because of what I felt in my cell that day.

I wrote to my mum and dad and I told them in my letter what had happened. My mum wrote back telling me that she was reading a book at this time by Pete Doherty's mother called, '*My Prodigal Son*'. So, God touched my heart that day in jail and Wilky who was just out of Carstairs was maybe used to things like this happening.

When the Bible fell the window was closed, there was no wind coming through the cell. I know it was God who made it fall and then open at that parable. Wilky was my only witness that this happened, but he can't remember a thing about it, but it did happen as God is my witness.

Chapter 83

I was sitting in our cell one night with Wilky, watching the Scottish news when we saw footage of Kenilworth Crescent. A taxi driver had been murdered on my old street (*Hole Farm Road*). Both mine and Wilky's first custodial sentences were for knifing guys in Kenilworth. He was sentenced to four years when he was 15 and I was sentenced to two and a half when I was 17. We were also both patients in Carstairs. I visited him on a special visit because I was a former patient. We weren't allowed to make contact with each other. Now we were both locked up together viewing a TV transmission of a taxi driver murdered on my street, just along from my old house.

The murderer was envious that his ex-girlfriend went away with someone else (*who was a taxi driver*). So, he hired his love rival's car and told him to drive and while he was being driven through Hole Farm Road, jealousy drove the killer to stabbing his taxi driver to death.

When the killer was found guilty, he faked a heart attack in the dock at the High Court. He then got jailed for life, a minimum of 14 years for his efforts.

In later years, another murder happened on the second of my old streets in Greenock, after I lived there. A man was stabbed to death on Maple Road in front of his two children. The police arrested a man missing his front and bottom teeth. This killer was ruthless and toothless.

Chapter 84

This time Wilky was doing six years and nine months for a danger of life and permanent disability. He stabbed a man behind the knee, and the man lost a limb. Surgeons had to amputate one of the man's legs to save his life due to the damage done. There was even a TV programme about it. There was a story about it, but neither me nor Wilky has ever seen it, but Andy watched it while he was in jail.

On the night of the attack, Wilky was in a pub drinking with his cousin, then at midnight he went to a cash machine to check his accounts balance as he was due to be paid on that day, but his payment wasn't in his account. A man cycled past on his bike. He used the cash machine, then Wilky stabbed him in the leg with a sharp knife. Wilky then went to the mental ward in Greenock and told staff he was hearing voices, but he was sent away from the hospital. Weeks later surgeons had to amputate the man's leg to save his life. Wilky told me about it at a visit in Gateside on Christmas Eve.

The bank machine was a free cash line. There was no extra charge to withdraw money, but this victim had to pay and it cost him an arm and a leg.

Before Wilky was jailed for attempted murder he was involved in another attempted murder too, but he never got caught. Donza went to jail instead. Donza knew that it was Wilky who did it, but he kept his mouth shut and went to jail for 110 days.

On the night of the attack they walked into Donza's house where they found a man sitting drinking in his living room. Wilky stabbed the man and battered him with a wooden guitar. Wilky then went back to Greenock. Donza went to Greenock too, in the back of a reliance van to Gateside prison.

Wilky went and visited Donza in jail where he told him that he would take the blame and then plead insanity, but Wilky stabbed someone else and was then jailed where he shared a cell with Donza. Wilky played the mental health card and was sent to Carstairs.

Donza got out. Wilky didn't take the blame, but he walked free and he wasn't singing. He said, "No comment" all the way. There was just no evidence against him. He spent five months in jail for striking a man on the body with a knife or similar instrument and striking him on the head with a guitar or similar instrument. Donza looked instrumental, even though he went to jail his nature was gentle. Wilky looked mental.

Chapter 85

One day I phoned my mum from Barlinnie and she told me that I had been offered a house in Bridge of Weir. My mum thought that it was a mistake because of similarities. The address of my family home was Hillview, Bridge of Weir Road, Kilmacolm and the flat that I was getting offered was Hillview Road, Bridge of Weir.

After confusion, my dad phoned up the Johnstone Housing Association. He told the housing officer that I was in jail but he would pay the rent upfront, so that I could get the house upon my release, but it was a no go and I lost this flat which made me anxious.

I thought that I would never get another house in Bridge of Weir because I was in jail doing a sentence, had a warrant out for my arrest, so wasn't expecting to get out.

One day Wilky asked me if I knew anyone who we could both write to. I told him that I always wrote to a girl called Lynsay whenever I was in jail. Wilky asked me what Lynsay's second name was and when I told him he laughed and told me that was his cousin. I didn't know this. I was writing to Lynsay for two years (*whenever I came to jail*) and she would write back. Wilky had bought A4 paper in Carstairs so we wrote a letter to his cousin. He wrote on one side of the paper and I wrote on the other. Three or four days later a letter came back it was from her.

She gave us her phone number and we phoned from Barlinnie. Lynsay asked Wilky if she could visit him so I came up with an idea. I told Wilky that when I got out, I would bring Lynsay to visit him and he agreed that my plan was a good one.

We wrote a letter to Lynsay telling her what we thought and she wrote back telling us she was up for it. A week before I was getting out Wilky booked a visit for me and Lynsay to come and see him. Another visit confirmation slip came through our cell door with mine and Lynsay's names on it. Our visit had been granted and I wasn't even out yet!

My liberation date was a Friday, but I had a warrant out for my arrest, so I was expecting to get arrested. I thought the police would detain me and take me to the police station for the whole weekend until court on Monday where I would get jailed again.

I hoped I would get out because I knew what I was going to do. I wanted to visit Wilky again with Lynsay too.

Chapter 86

The police couldn't have known I was in Barlinnie because even though there was a warrant for my arrest, I got out on Good Friday 2008. Then two days later, on Easter Sunday, I met up with Lynsey and we went to the Holiday Inn in Greenock where we spent the night drinking.

On the following Thursday, Lynsey came to Kilmacolm and my mum ran us to Barlinnie to visit Wilky. We had a good visit, then we left Wilky in Barlinnie and went back to Kilmacolm. I spent the next week with Lynsey and we were together every day.

On the Sunday after Easter, Lynsey asked me if I would take her to Church with me, but I told her that I would take her some other time, so we never went. I was with her every day for a full week. We visited Wilky in Barlinnie on the Thursday. On the following Thursday, Lynsey went home but we arranged that I was going to see her again on the Sunday.

Lynsey phoned me on the Friday and Saturday and we were texting each other over the weekend too. On the Saturday night, I went to my sister's old house in Gallowhill, Paisley and spent the night there.

When I got to my sister's, I had two text messages from Lynsey. One of them said that she couldn't see me and the other one said, sorry.

The next day I went back to Kilmacolm and I got wine with another boy. While I was walking up the stairs of my close, I could hear my house phone ringing and I thought it might be Wilky phoning from jail. I ran in through my front door and answered the phone, and it was Wilky. I told him about me and Lynsey being together every day since our visit. We spoke for a while as I drank my wine, then Wilky had to go back in his cell, so our conversation ended.

I drank some more then the phone rang for the second time. At first, I thought it might be Wilky again but as it turned out it wasn't. The words the woman said before she hung up, rang in my head. *"Lynsey is dead"*.

Chapter 87

L ynsey died. I thought it was a tragic accident. Wilky told me that if Lynsey was with me the night she died, then she would still be alive and if I never got myself the jail to keep him company, then he would never have seen her again. Because I wrote to her from jail, Wilky got to see his cousin one last time through me and my letters. Although, if I hadn't got myself jailed on purpose, then I would never have been with her either. The whole time I was with Lynsey I had a warrant out for my arrest and I expected to get arrested but I never. I got out and met up with her on Easter.

At this time, me, Lynsey and Wilky were all 22 years old and she had a wee son. The police came to see me because she spent the last week of her life with me. They asked me questions about her, but I didn't tell them anything.

I was told that I wasn't allowed to go to the funeral because I was evil. I hadn't carried a knife for over two years, but my past haunted me. I could go and see her body, but I never went. At the day of the funeral my brother took me to her grave. We found it no bother in a huge cemetery. We drove right to it, like we already knew where it was.

I phoned up Barlinnie and told the screws that Wilky's cousin had died but they wouldn't take my word for it so I had to give them details and wait until they contacted the Greenock police to find out for sure. Then they got a priest to tell him because Wilky is a Catholic.

Wilky couldn't believe it because me and Lynsey were only up visiting him over a week before she died. She told me that when Wilky got out, she would take him in and look after him and keep him out of trouble.

Wilky's letters were buried in with her and I can't help but wonder if mine were too? After all, we both wrote to her on different sides of Wilky's A4 paper which he had bought in Carstairs.

All I wanted was to go back to jail, so I got the bus to Stirling to smash up the police station. When I found the police building, I smashed a brick through the window, then I walked into the cop shop to face the coppers. I was ran at and grabbed, then thrown in a cell where an hour later I was given fish and chips. The next day after breakfast in bed I was taken to Stirling Sheriff Court and put in the cells. A few hours later they opened me up and told me that I had been given a PF's release but was being detained under warrant for apprehension.

The reliance van took me back to the Stirling police station via the women's prison. There were female prisoners getting dropped off at HMP Cornton Vale. Later that night I was moved to Greenock police station until court the next day. I was going to plead guilty to get myself sent to prison. I didn't want to get out.

I was given another four months for threatening to stab an 18-year-old boy and resisting arrest. I was in for two months and got out for five weeks then I was back in for another two months. I wanted to go back to Barlinnie to share a cell with Wilky again and I tried to (*again*) but I never made it. I never got jailed at the Stirling Court, I was taken to jail from Greenock. I was back to the worst jail (*Gateside*).

A boy I used to share a cell with was in the court cells with me and he told me that Darroch Hall in Gateside had been changed to a young offender's unit. I was 22 but the jail computer thought I was 21, so I hatched a plan. When I went into the reception, I got a screw to change my date of birth again by making me appear to be another year younger. I lied again and said I was 20. The jail believed me again and I was classed as a YO (*two times over*). I then asked the screws in Ailsa Hall to move me to the YO hall.

My plan worked and I was seen as a YO and put in the young offender's unit. My head was fried and I wasn't thinking clearly. All I really wanted was to go back to Barlinnie. That was my real plan, but it never worked and I ended up in Greenock jail (*plan B*).

When I got arrested for this offence, I had a knife on me, but I threw it away and the police never found it. I was aggressive and they beat me up, bursting my head open and I was taken to the hospital where the medical staff sent me back to the police station for the night.

The next day I was taken to court where I was bailed, but I never appeared back at court on the later date because I was in prison.

A warrant was granted for my arrest, but the police couldn't have realised that I was in Barlinnie and I got back out.

I wanted to stab this boy in his girlfriend's house, but she phoned the police on me. Then along with her boyfriend they both signed statements against me claiming that I was trying to break into the house. I got arrested and later jailed for four months.

Luckily for me the police never found my blade and luckily for the informer I never got into his girlfriend's house that night. I was out to commit a knife crime. I never cared about the jail time.

Chapter 88

My head was all over the place and I wasn't thinking clearly. I never made it to B-Hall Barlinnie, I got myself put into the YO hall in Gateside. All I wanted was to go back to Barlinnie.

Plan B worked and I was put into the YO hall, but four days later I got moved to Polmont. I never ever thought that this would happen but Polmont broke me. I didn't love it at all anymore. When I was a YO I really enjoyed it, but I must have grown up since Barlinnie because I felt Polmont had become such a dire place. I didn't like it at all anymore. Now I hated it.

I told the screws that I was 22 but they didn't believe me. They told me to prove it by getting my birth certificate sent in. I phoned my mum and she photocopied my birth lines and posted it into me with a clipping of me in the newspaper named and shamed, but age given.

The Greenock Telegraph said that I was a thug who terrorised a family and that I was remanded, but there were only two people in the house, no family. I got jailed for four months not remanded.

I was in a single cell in Monro Hall. There were four floors all kept apart from each other and I was on the bottom flat. Cramond Hall had been knocked down and all the protections were up on Monro top flat. At night-time, boys from all the flats would shout abuse from their cell windows at the protections on floor four.

One night I heard some boys shouting at a convicted murderer, who was serving 20 years to life for murdering his 14-year-old girl-friend when he was also 14. *"Luke Mitchell is innocent, he is innocent"* the boys were shouting. I was lying in a single cell locked up in the same building as this apparent killer who I knew would be in a single cell as well. I knew that he would be able to hear the ranting.

In later years this convicted murderer passed a polygraph lie detector test claiming to be innocent and at his trial the evidence against him was all circumstantial. He still pleads his innocence to the end. I'm sorry I don't want to offend, but I wonder if he did kill his girlfriend.

Chapter 89

My mum got my birth certificate photocopied and sent me a duplicate copy through the mail to Polmont. I was then told that I was going to Barlinnie. I felt relieved because I liked Barlinnie and my days of loving Polmont were over. I hated it now.

Before I left Polmont, I was prescribed antipsychotic medica-tion which made me go out like a light. When I got to Barlinnie, I told the screws what had happened to Wilky's cousin asking them if I could go back into the same cell with him. When I got to B-Hall he had just been given a new co-pilot, but the screws put me in the cell next door to him. I would shout through the wall and talk to Wilky. We both got opened up at the same time for dinner and would also stand in the medication queue. We were both prescribed the same medication (*olanzapine*).

A few days later Wilky got moved to Glenochil. After this the screws sent me over to D-Hall, to the mental unit. I was pleased to go to the small unit with a single cell.

About a week later I got my Saturday morning paper and I saw with my own eyes a terrible tragedy. Blaney had drowned. He was in the water in Loch Lomond and swam in after a ball and he was sucked under and it cost him his life. I drank with Blaney loads of times and since he died Bridge of Weir seems strange without him.

His best friend Paul couldn't understand why Blaney had to drown. In return he continued to drown his own sorrows. Paul couldn't handle that him and Blaney were apart and sometimes time doesn't heal a broken heart.

Chapter 90

I saw Paul one time in Bridge of Weir and he could hardly walk. It was a shame. He came staggering out of the weir and we walked along the viaduct. He was fishing, but he never caught anything. I told Paul he was going to die and he shrugged his shoulders. He didn't care.

I finally managed to get off drink and I was going to different Churches. My heart bled for Paul. I walked past a bench where Auld's bakers used to be. I had met Paul and Blaney there loads of times. Paul was sitting staring into space he was totally lost. I gave him money and cigarettes and he bought a bottle of cider with it and we went and sat under a different bridge at the old railway station. Paul cried for Blaney and he said he wished that he was with him. I didn't know what to say, then he told me he wished that he was there to save him. I told Paul that he would have went with him and he told me that's what he wanted. I realised that poor Paul had a death wish and I hoped that he would come out of it but he never.

A few months later Paul died (*on the day that would've been Blaney's 21st birthday*). It happened in the house that I got offered when I was in jail. Paul drank every day with Blaney but after Blaney died he went into complete self-destruction.

I heard people used to find Paul sleeping on Blaney's grave when they went to put flowers down. Paul didn't know how to pay his respects, he was too far gone.

Seven months later Yogi passed away. He went to jail for a few months and came out, then overdosed a few days later and died on Halloween.

Before he died, I had seen him sitting wrecked with his head rolling down his body and I would joke with him asking him what day he thought it was (*Halloween*), because he was dooking for apples! When he was straight, he found it funny, but now it is no laughing matter.

Yogi and Blaney never knew each other. They met through me and along with Paul, the four of us got drunk one day in Bridge of Weir. Now they are all dead except me. All gone before their time. It's like I'm the sole survivor with a tragic tale to tell.

That day Paul went to see his lawyer and with Yogi and Blaney we started walking to Kilmacolm, where Blaney and Yogi ended up face to face nearly fighting, near Quarriers on the cycle track. Yogi punched Blaney which made him turn around and go back to Bridge of Weir in a huff. Me and Yogi walked to the Pullman pub in Kilmacolm.

Paul was cremated and his ashes were scattered along the weir, where he walked up that day. Blaney and Yogi are buried back to back in Kilbarchan cemetery, their gravestones are behind each other. They never even knew each other. They met through me and now their remains are left together.

Yogi died on Halloween 2009 and on Halloween 2019 I went to his grave with flowers. I bought two bouquets, for both Blaney and Yogi's graves. I put both the flowers along the top of their gravestones back to back and I left them touching each other. I know the wind may have blown them over, but I did this in respect of them both.

Paul was 24 when he died and I heard that it was a heart attack that killed him. Everyone knew his heart was broken, but to die on the day that was Blaney's 21st Heavenly birthday, I don't care what anyone says, I think he died from a broken heart. Now Paul and Blaney are together again and I proclaim that Bridge of Weir will never ever be the same (*what a shame*).

Chapter 91

When I was in jail doing five months, I was back in Barlinnie again. I was moved over to D-Hall (*south upper*) and there was a celebrity prisoner in the hall, a professional boxer and former world champion, Scott Harrison.

One morning the guy I was sharing a cell with, went out into the section to ask the screws if we could go for a shower. When he came back, he told me that he thought someone had been stabbed. Our door was then locked and we never got a shower. The screws then came back, searched our cell and locked us up on a rule. We were then blamed of slashing and stabbing another prisoner. We were ruled up for three days and articles appeared in the country's newspapers.

The guy who got carved up was mouthing off telling anyone who would listen that if anyone touched Scott Harrison, then he would carve them up. The prisoner who listened, carved him up and then apparently blamed me. The screws told me that the other prisoner was blaming me. I was also told that the police were coming to see me, but I refused to talk to them.

Articles appeared in the newspapers stating that a lag who claimed to be the former world champion's minder had been knifed in his cell. After three days we were cleared as we never done it.

My mum always said that boxing was too vicious and she nearly bumped into Mike Tyson. Years ago, when Tyson was fighting at Braehead Arena my mum and wee sister went shopping to Braehead. My mum nearly walked right into him. My mum had asked me if I wanted to go shopping with her and my sister, but I never went with them. If I had I would have seen the former world champion.

When the prisoner got attacked the screws told me I had to talk to the police. I refused to talk to them. I remained silent. Maybe my mum's right and boxing is too violent.

Chapter 92

On Lynsey's first memorial, I went to her grave with flowers, where I met her mum again. I never went back to jail and went to Lynsey's grave for the next two years on her memorial. On the fourth year I was back in jail.

When I got out, I went to Lynsey's grave on her fifth memorial with a girl who knew her. I hadn't had any medication for about three years and I kept all Lynsey's letters. I was drunk every day and got a tattoo on my arm. It was Lynsey's handwriting (*arms of an angel*).

I went to the Glasgow High Court to watch a murder trial. A boy I knew was accused of murder and his aunt had a tattoo that said, 'arms of an angel'. When I went home, I played the lyrics on YouTube and the words of the song made me think of Lynsey because we went to a 'dark cold hotel room' in Easter.

The murder trial that I watched was concluded on Halloween which was the day of sentencing. I went to Yogi's grave with flowers, then I went to the High Court in Glasgow where I watched a 19-year-old boy get sentenced to life imprisonment. He got 15 years for his efforts.

On Lynsey's sixth memorial, my mum took me to her grave and I said I wondered if anything would happen that day that I could put in this book. That night I went on Facebook where I noticed that Paddy's brother, posted Wilky's mobile phone number on it. Then I decided to phone it.

Wilky had written me a 'dear john' letter because he thought that being in contact with me might dent his chances of getting out. So, I hadn't spoken to him for nearly three years. I phoned him and spoke for a while and we arranged to meet up. I told him it was

Lynsey's memorial. We spoke about going to her grave together, but Wilky wasn't allowed to go because he was banned from Inverclyde for the foreseeable future. As time went on, I hadn't seen Wilky for another three years, then I texted him one Saturday night to see how he was doing. He texted me a message back telling me that his dad has just died.

Although I hadn't seen him for ages, I planned to go to his father's funeral, but without telling him. I was just going to turn up out of the blue, so I bought the Greenock Telegraph every day looking through the column on local deaths but there wasn't anything listed any day. Then on Facebook a memory came up on my profile of a picture of me and Wilky (*5 years before*).

At that time, I decided to text Wilky asking him when his dad's funeral was so that I definitely wouldn't miss it and he replied, "tomorrow". So, the next day I went to Wilky's dad's funeral in a chapel in Greenock. After the service, Wilky's dad was taken to the Greenock Cemetery and was buried in with Lynsey.

Wilky had never been to her grave before this, but he carried his dad's coffin to the final place of rest. So, me and Wilky did make it to Lynsey's grave together, but he had to bury his father in the process.

Lynsey's mum gave me a cuddle at the graveside and I saw Lynsey's son again. Wilky took a cord lowering his dad's coffin down into the plot in the grave.

On the night of his dad's funeral, I texted him to see how he was and Wilky texted me back telling me that one of his dogs died 10 minutes after he got back from the funeral. His Staffy took a heart attack. Wilky told me he was close to losing it, so I prayed for peace of mind for him. After all he didn't want to go back to jail or mental hospitals.

After Lynsey died, Wilky left Barlinnie's B-Hall, went down the mental health route again and was sent back to Carstairs for years. He was doing six years, nine months, but after his liberation date he was kept for years.

Wilky was the heaviest smoker I knew and then he ended up with cancer, but he fought the battle and survived. Although he had to do years in mental institutions, he could have done over four years and got out the jail, but he had to do over seven (six *years in mental institutions*).

I know that I didn't really know Lynsey and some people say that it was just a fling that we had. Maybe they are absolutely right. People go on holiday for a week or two and meet someone they like while they are away. That's the way I feel about the time I had with Lynsey. Like we were both on holiday, after all we started it off in the Holiday Inn on the Easter holiday.

Easter Sunday is about Jesus Christ dying and coming back to life and when I was with Lynsey, I played the Pink Floyd song *Coming Back To Life* and she loved it. Although Easter is about the resurrection of Jesus, after Lynsey died, I always thought about her at Easter time. In doing my research, I found out that in the year 2042 her memorial (*6th April*) will be on Easter Sunday. The question is, will I be alive to see it?

Chapter 93

I met a guy outside who I had heard about when I was in jail. Lynchy, was jailed for six years for a knife attack and while he was serving his time he slashed and stabbed other prisoners. He was moved to a special unit in Perth prison to house Scotland's most dangerous prisoners. While he was inside the prison (*within a prison*) he stabbed Robert M in the back and stomach. Lynchy was charged for this attack and the Carstairs escapee stood up at trial and gave evidence against him. Lynchy, was found guilty and sentenced to serve more time in jail, but because of the crimes that the criminally insane victim had committed, Lynchy wasn't jailed for very much longer and he told me it was worth it, but his time in jail wasn't all fun and games.

I stayed with his brother in their family home in Port Glasgow and Lynchy invited me to join him in his room. I went to his own house in Bouverie Street as well in the same town. I saw him in jail in Barlinnie's B-Hall and then when he got out, he moved to Greenock. On Boxing Day 2010 his front door was kicked in and he was hit about the head with a metal object. He was in hospital for a few days then he signed himself out on New Year's Eve. I don't think he took it well and after discharging himself from hospital, on the 2nd of January 2011, his body packed up and Lynchy died.

After his death, his mum told me that she found homemade rosary beads which her late son had made in his flat. Lynchy couldn't go on another day. He was cremated in the Greenock Crematorium and his ashes were scattered in the grounds of Saint Francis of Assisi Chapel in Port Glasgow.

Robert M (*who has done a lot of damage to different people including murder*) complained to the police that Lynchy stabbed him. I always hated police informers and after the stabbing he was in the court blabbing.

Chapter 94

Back when I was in Polmont in 2003, I watched the news one night and I saw a girl who got jailed for life for murder. I liked the look of her and thought about writing to her but didn't. Four years later I saw her in the newspapers again and decided that I would write to her. I was outside at this time.

Gemma was 17 years old when she got jailed for life. I told her in my letter that I thought she was dead pretty (*joke - do you get it?*) and in under a week she wrote back. After being pen-pals for a few months I was invited up to Cornton Vale for a visit, but I went to jail twice so we had to wait.

The same day I met Gemma she asked me to kiss her, then after I did, I ended up back in jail when the boxer escapade happened.

At this time, I watched a programme on the TV called *Girls Behind Bars* and I saw Gemma on it and this made me want to kiss her again even more. I fancied her from the start.

As the years went on, I went to Cornton Vale more and more to see Gemma, until we ended up falling in love with each another. After all I've been through, I suppose it was fate that made me fall in love in a prison visit room. We got engaged and then married as well on home leaves.

I got a 'Gemma' tattoo on my arm and then Gemma got a dream catcher tattoo on her arm with 'Nathan' in the middle. Before I proposed to Gemma, I got her engagement ring finger sized and the correct size was *N* – for ***Nathan***.

I first wrote to Gemma in 2007 and I have been visiting her ever since I met her in 2008. Eight years later (*2015*) she came out on home-leaves to my flat every month for a week at a time. We had our first Christmas together and then Gemma's 30th birthday on different home leaves.

Love was in the air and Gemma fell pregnant. Our baby was conceived on a home leave. My brother's girlfriend was pregnant at the same time too. And my niece was born – Penelope, but disaster struck. I had my urine screened at Dykebar APC (*alcohol problems clinic*) and I failed for cocaine, a few different times and the nurses told the social work department who then stopped Gemma's home leaves to my house.

The jail let her out for nine hours to marry me, but then Gemma had to go back to jail and finish her life sentence before our baby was born. When most people get married, they spend their wedding night with their lover, but my bride went back to jail. We never had any honeymoon; she went back to prison.

I'm not glad that a man lost his life, but if Gemma didn't get jailed for life then she wouldn't be in my life and now we have a love life. We made a life and the Church we got married in was called Life.

My mum and dad's old Church used to be called Living Word but then the name changed to Life Church. Our Pastor married us in the old building in Paisley.

Our baby was conceived on a Christmas home leave in my old flat in Bridge of Weir and on 22nd September 2016 my son was born - Nathan. Baby Nathan was born in Wishaw General Hospital and so was my niece too. Not much chance of this happening, considering me and my brother are both from Kilmacolm, but it's how it did happen.

We married in secret so the media wouldn't find out, but over a year later we were in the newspapers. Journalists came to my mum and dad's door looking for me to give a story on Gemma, but I refused. So, the press went on my Facebook and took pictures of our wedding day and blasted them across the newspaper.

I didn't think I could have children, but I prayed to God for me and Gemma to have a son and about a week later she told me she was pregnant. I prayed every day that our baby would be a boy. Even before he was born, we took him to Church in his mother's womb. After all, he was conceived in my old flat which was Church Road (*at Christmas time*) and as we all know, Jesus was born on Christmas.

It's mad how that when I was younger, I wanted to get myself a lifer. And now I have one - Gemma xxx.

Chapter 95

All my so-called friends let me down. They didn't want to know me unless it benefited them. None of them were there for me when I needed them, they just used me for whatever they could get from me.

One day, one of these friends phoned my family home to speak to me and I answered and took her call. She told me that she was parked outside in her mum's car, so I went down to see her. She was sitting in the back with her boyfriend and she told me to get

141

in the front, so I got in and sat beside her mum who was driving.

I was then lured to show her where a man stayed. I never knew what actual house the man lived in, but I always saw him at the park with his dog. So, we went to the park and the man was there with his pet. The girl, then told me that this man touched her sister up. This was a predicament and I never fell for it. I sat in the front seat of a car and I took a back seater. I was off the drink a year and I had stopped carrying a knife and now I was getting used first of all to show them roughly where the man stayed, but now they wanted me to attack a man in his 60s.

I never done it and neither did they. Although they fired other people in and they went to the wrong door and got the wrong man. An old man in his 70s was knifed and battered, while he was robbed of his savings.

My apparent friend and her mum talked other people into going to attack and rob a man in his late 60s but the attackers got the wrong old man. Then my friend's mum *(who was the getaway driver)* turned Queen's evidence and got one of the guys jailed for life.

There were three attackers who did the robbery, but the informer didn't inform on the other two people. She picked on this one guy and gave evidence against him and now he's in jail serving life. This one guy was picked out of the three assailants and thrown to the wolves, but that's what they always do. They pick their victims every time and would all rat on their granny to save their own skin.

If I had got out of the car that day and attacked the man, at least I would have got the right man and not an even older man by mistake, but I refused to do any old man. Although I know that if I had done it, then I would be in jail doing life for a despicable act at the behest of my phony friend.

Whenever I hear about the robbery and attempted murder of the old man in Kilmacolm I always think that it could have been me. For years, this friend was up at court every week or two for a string of charges every time, but none of the judges ever sentenced her to a single prison sentence. She walked out of court constantly after pleading guilty.

She was never a witness in a courtroom, but she orchestrated evidence from behind the scenes and along with her mother and sister they had to leave the country because they informed on every Tom, Dick and Harry.

My pretend friend wanted me to write about how close we were, but I'm not naming her in this book because she is spineless. I call her super grass, super glue, because she's stuck that many people in. She doesn't deserve to be named (*but shamed*).

Chapter 96

I was off the drink for three months and I suddenly had a compulsion to drink. I went to the shops to get a bottle, but before I reached the Cross a boy who lived nearby, pulled up in his car at his house.

This boy had ecstasy tablets in his living room locked away in a safe. I quickly changed my mind about drinking and I followed the boy into his house where I got some tablets. I never drank, I took ecstasy instead and I managed to stay off the drink for another year.

Then one morning the CID came to my mum's house and arrested me from my bed and I was taken to the Greenock police station and charged with three serious assaults. Along with the boy who gave me ecstasy we were both charged for these attacks. When I got to the charge bar at the police station, I gave my name and address only, but dismissed a legal representative. When I was interviewed, I just said my usual catchphrase (*No Comment*).

I was charged with two assault to severe injury and permanent disfigurements and an assault to severe injury. Whilst acting with another, I was said to have punched and kicked two men on the head and body and hit another man on the head with a bottle.

At this point, it was the end of August 2010, but the attacks happened back in May of that year (three *months before*), so I was bailed under an undertaking, for two weeks and had to sign a promise that I would appear at court two weeks later.

Two days before I was due to attend a first pleading diet in the Greenock Sheriff Court, I went and bought a bottle of Buckfast. I was 15 months sober and when I opened the bottle, I knew that I was back in my addiction, but I didn't care. I thought I was going to get jailed only days later. I used to like being in jail for a few months at a time, but now I was facing years. I didn't want this anymore.

On the morning of court my mum woke me up and drove me to my first pleading diet. I was wanting to get a bottle beforehand but never got one. When I walked into the Greenock Sheriff Court, my lawyer told me that the PF had thrown my case out, that all the charges against us had been dropped. I walked free, but I wasn't free of addiction. I was trapped in my alcoholism. My mum told me that I'd drank for nothing and she was right, but now I was back on the wine every morning, noon and night.

Chapter 97

Because I became a drug addict at 15 my dad decided that he wanted to reach out and help other addicts. So, he volunteered and became the leader of an organisation in Paisley called Teen Challenge which has drug rehabilitation centres all over the world. I went to a rehab down the Scottish borders, but I left the next day.

The centre manager drove me to the train station at Berwick Upon Tweed. Before the train to Glasgow came, I walked to the shops and bought a bottle of wine and drank it, but then I had my regrets. I phoned my mum to ask her to phone the rehab to see if I could go back, but she never answered the phone. I then decided to pray. I asked God to show me a sign, should I try and go back to the rehab or should I get on the train to Glasgow, when it arrived. Instantly the phone in the train station rang. I quickly answered and it was my mum. She gave me the rehab's phone number and I phoned and asked if I could go back. The manager agreed and came and picked me up at the train station. He asked me to let him smell my breath which I did but he couldn't smell the drink off me because I ate a sandwich and brushed my teeth.

He took me back to the rehab, but I left the next day. This time I was taken to Edinburgh where I was dropped off at this other train station. Again, I walked to a shop where I bought another bottle of Buckfast that I drank while waiting for the train to Glasgow. I finished my bottle on the train.

My dad used to run a tea and coffee kitchen from one of the Teen Challenge buses and I would sometimes go with him on a Thursday night. Some weeks' Eggy would come on board and get a cuppa and something to eat.

One time I went with my dad and he stopped at Houston, on our way and bought me a chicken supper from the chippy. My dad parked his car at Paisley's Love Street in the car park behind the Teen Challenge bus. I ate my cooked chicken in the car. Then I went a walk up to the local pub to wash my hands as they were greasy.

While I was walking along the street, I saw a man swinging a girl about. Then I saw him pull something from his pocket so that he could hit her with it. As quick as I could, I grabbed the man and threw him to the ground. Then, as quick as anything, I heard a click, turned around to see what the noise was. A man bounced in at me and then away again. Just at that same moment, I felt wind brushing past my neck. I then saw that the man had a knife and I felt a nip on my neck. This guy had tried to slash my throat. It turned out that the man I had thrown to the ground was his dad.

I challenged the man to fight and he flew at me with his lock back but before he could get in any closer, I pulled out a knife and he backed off. I then told him he was lucky he'd made the right decision and he bolted.

I was lucky I even had a knife on me because I'd stopped carrying them. I only had a blade that night so that I could cut up my chicken supper. I should have left it in my dad's car but somehow, I took it out with me. I suppose a part of me wanted to use it and I know that really, I was the lucky one.

I went to a rehab centre near Aberdeen, but I left the next day. I didn't even give it a chance. I walked out, but I remember a member of staff who worked there. Then one Thursday night, I saw him on the Teen Challenge bus in Paisley.

Along with my dad, we arranged to go up to Aberdeenshire to go out on their Teen Challenge bus. So, we did. Me and my dad stayed with my aunt and uncle in Tarves, while we were up there.

I helped out on the bus, making drug addicts tea and coffee. Then journalists from the local newspaper appeared and took a photo of us and an article appeared in the Aberdeenshire newspaper making it look like I was a full time Teen Challenge helper.

We never knew that the newspaper reporters were even coming. They surprisingly appeared out of the blue. Funny that I used to love being in the newspapers for violence and being bad. Then, unexpectedly with my dad, I'm in the newspaper for doing good (*near my aunt's neighbourhood*).

Chapter 98

One night, Neil turned up at my mum and dad's door wanting me to hide him after he'd been stabbed to bits but my dad wouldn't let him stay, so I took him to my flat in Bridge of Weir where me and Neil stayed for a few weeks. When he left, I didn't see him again until I saw him in jail.

Neil was institutionalised. He couldn't handle life on the outside. He coped better when he was in jail. He was a violent criminal but sometimes he would manage to stay out for months at a time, but he never stopped offending, he just never got caught for every offence. He was addicted to drink and drugs. He needed different substances to get through each day. I came across him at a Church meeting in Greenock where we both ate a meal prepared for us by Christians. I told Neil that God could change his life, but he wasn't interested. He just wanted the free food at the meal and message.

I never saw him again, then a year later I woke up one morning, checked my mobile phone, where there was a text message from Patman (early that morning) that told me Neil was dead. He died in a flat in Greenock. Not long before he died, he fell and broke his back. Then he got stabbed again and social workers wouldn't let him see his baby son. I think Neil went into self-destruction.

Years ago, my dad prayed for him and he cried his eyes out while my dad was praying for him. At one point, Neil told me that he thought about becoming a Christian.

Neil was the best car thief that I ever knew. He was an expert at stealing old Corsa's. I was with him one day when he stole a Corsa. He bent the car door open with his fingers, then once inside he snapped the steering lock, ripped the casing off the ignition barrel and started the car with my house key, then we were off to Kilmacolm. Whilst he was driving up the backroads he crashed into another car, so he ditched the stolen car in Port Glasgow's Moray Road. My wallet fell out my pocket in the car with my bank card and my provisional driving licence inside.

I was later asked by a policeman where my provisional was and I told him the truth. I lost it, which I did, but what I didn't admit was where. On the first ever night that I was with him (*on the outside*), he came to Kilmacolm and picked me up in a stolen car. He told me he was coming in a red Corsa and then he appeared in a white Corsa. He was driving the red car to Kilmacolm, but he ran out of petrol, so he stopped and stole another white car, before he picked me up. I knew it was stolen cars, but I didn't mind. I thought Neil was colour blind!

Chapter 99

I became a mess on the drink and wanted to go back to jail to get off it. I went to Glasgow to get myself arrested. I walked into one of the police stations where the floor had just been mopped. I picked up the wet floor sign and threw it at the charge bar where the police officers were. I was arrested and then taken to the hospital to be examined by a mental health doctor.

I was deemed fit to be locked in a cell, so I was taken back to the police station for the night. The next day, I was taken to Glasgow Sheriff Court where I was wanting to go back to Barlinnie, but I was given a PF's release and got out. I was gutted. I wanted to go get jailed but failed.

I stayed out of jail for nearly three years, but then the helicopter caught me. The police captured me on the cycle track in Kilmacolm right next to the ashes. It was a dark Wednesday night at the end of February 2012.

The police helicopter was flying all over me circling the area. I knew I was getting arrested. The police came running at me, screaming at me to lie down flat on my face. I was handcuffed from behind and held down for about an hour while the police searched the track for weapons.

I could feel the police dogs smelling me and I could sense they were sniffing me. I was then picked up and carted from the track and thrown into the back of a police jail wagon. I was then taken to Paisley police station. I hadn't spoken a word to police since I got arrested and when I got to the charge bar I still refused to speak. I was stripped naked and shoved into a cell with the iron door slammed in my face.

I lay on the mat drunk, totally naked. I was cold, but I just lay there and felt relieved. I was glad I was in. I knew I was going to jail and I missed it.

I didn't know how long I was going to prison for because I didn't know what the charge was. All I knew was that if I made myself suffer then things could only get better.

A while later the cell door was opened and the cop shop janny left a blanket for me and I felt cozy. Because I never spoke, the police got a psychiatric doctor to come and have a look at me, but I never communicated with him either. The doctor told the police that I had bipolar and that I was fine.

My lawyer walked into the cell and told me to say, 'No Comment'. The Paisley CID then came and took me from my cell to the interview room to question me. They gave me shorts and a T-shirt to wear through my interview. I had a duty solicitor by my side for legal advice, on the grounds of my own lawyer, who had arranged for him to guide me. I was put through a viper parade and questioned. I said, 'No Comment' to everything and was charged with assault to severe injury.

The next day was Friday and I was taken to court, but not with all the other hold ins. The police had taken my clothes from me as they had blood on them. I had nothing to wear, so the police had to clothe me.

The Paisley CID went to Asda and bought me George clothes to wear to court. The only words I spoke in those two days, after my lawyer's advice, was, 'No Comment' about five times. I was taken to Paisley Sheriff Court in handcuffs by the CID at lunchtime. I was put in a court cell. I saw my lawyer and he told me I would be getting remanded because I was under petition and that I would be getting served another indictment. So, by law I couldn't apply for bail. When I appeared in court, I was remanded for seven days as no plea of declaration.

I was taken to Barlinnie and held in the first night centre for the weekend. On Monday, I was moved to C-Hall remand. On the following Friday, I was taken back to court. My lawyer told me that there was a very slim chance I would get bail because of my previous convictions for violence, so I would need special circumstances for a judge to bail me out.

I was meant to be going to rehab in Northern Ireland, but I never asked for bail. I wanted to stay in jail and rehabilitate myself.

I was remanded for a further 110 days. I never cared I was glad. I didn't want to get out. Not yet. I made a prayer that I would get out for Christmas, so I had my head set on that.

I wanted to plead guilty there and then to assault to severe injury, but my lawyer told me not to. He told me to wait until I had finished my full committal so that he could get the charge reduced. I took my solicitor's advice and did another, 'full commando'. I went back to Barlinnie's C-Hall for the next month.

In the police station, you are kept in solitary confinement and I never uttered a single solitary word for two days. Before I attacked the boy, he tried to run, then afterword I got arrested and done. The police wanted me to talk and co-operate, but they got none. It wasn't even a silent cell they had me in, but I made it one.

Chapter 100

Barlinnie's mental health team wanted me to move from C-Hall to the jail's psychiatric section. I refused to go at first, but then I decided to go for the single cell and the gym every day, plus I was guaranteed a daily shower.

I was moved over to D-Hall to the high dependency unit (*HDU*) which was known by other prisoners as the 'half daft unit' as the prisoners were either stupid or crazy. HDU was the SPS (*Scottish Prison Service*) stepping-stone to Carstairs. I already knew some of the guys from in there and some who I never knew, were on their way to the State Hospital.

HMP Barlinnie is the only jail in Scotland with a mental institution within the prison. People who have never been in jail call Barlinnie, 'Bar-L', but the guys who have been prisoners inside

150

Barlinnie, call the prison, Bar HDU. It is a nuthouse in Bar. I call it the nuthouse bar.

I started going to the gym every weekday, then rested at the weekend. I got quite big lifting weights but six weeks later, I was moved to the new Low Moss prison in Bishopbriggs, also in Glasgow. HMP Low Moss was a brand-new jail and I was put down the bottom flat of Kelvin House for remand prisoners.

Kelvin bottom flat was opened on Tuesday 1st May 2012 and I was moved from the nuthouse bar on Wednesday 2nd May. I was the first person to go into my cell. I was in the new jail with Eggy and he asked me would my dad come and see him. My dad visited him in the new jail.

About a month later, I went back to court. My lawyer got the charge reduced from assault to severe injury, to assault to an injury and I pled guilty. I shouldn't have been fully committed for 110 days as the injuries were minor. I only burst the boy's nose, bruised one of his eyes, bruised his jaw, and made a small laceration to his other eye.

My lawyer got me the deal on less injuries, but I had to plead guilty to hitting the boy on the head with a beer can which I never did. I took the deal and I put my hands up pleading guilty to punching and kicking a 19 year old boy on the head and body, knocking him to the ground and striking him on the head with a can of beer.

The judge put the case back for supervised release order reports. My remand continued and I went back to jail for another three weeks. When I returned to court the judge was off on the sick, so I was held on remand for another two weeks until the judge came back. I was taken back to Paisley Sheriff Court two weeks later and my lawyer told me that I was getting jailed for at least 18 months. I would be getting out to be monitored under another supervision order and the shortest sentence you could get would be 18 months. I was looking at 18 months or over. If I got longer, I would miss Christmas.

The judge was fit and well and away on his holidays, so a different judge sentenced me there and then to 12 months in jail with a full back dater and I never got put under another supervision order. So, the four months that I had done on remand came off my sentence. I had only two months left to serve. I only got nine months for the attack but three months for breaking a bail act.

I was sentenced to a year in jail at the Paisley Sheriff Court. The boy who I attacked, signed a statement telling police that I hit him on the head with a can of beer and that I punched and kicked him on the face because I blamed him for kicking in the front door of my house. He pressed assault charges against me, denying that he kicked my door in, but it was this boy who was so keen to deny attacking my door that brought the deservingness of this attack to light.

When I appeared in court the PF never referred to the boy as the victim always the complainer. I got a 12-month prison sentence and I never even hit him with a can of beer, it was someone else. But the culprit incriminated me and I kept my mouth shut. I had to plead guilty (*for this other man*), I had to carry the can.

Chapter 101

I went back to Low Moss prison, but I was now convicted which meant that I was moved from Kelvin's bottom flat up to the second flat. I wouldn't say I really liked it, but the new jail was okay. Anyway, two months later I was back out. Within a week of my release the Greenock police came to my family home and read me my rights, telling me that I was put under an intervention warrant for carrying offensive weapons.

I was the first person in Kilmacolm to be under an intervention warrant, which was a new law that gave police the power to intervene, arrest me and by law are able to hold me for 12 hours while they check the perimeter for weapons.

I never spoke to police again whilst I was being read my rights and also the rights they had, to detain me under suspicion. Now there was intelligence that I carried weapons, after all these years. Why at this time?

A few months later, I was arrested from my flat in Bridge of Weir and taken to the police station. I never spoke to the arresting officers while I was driven to Paisley. I was held in a room surrounded by police, then I was taken to Govan police station.

When the police officers got me to the charge bar in Govan, I was asked what nationality I was. I never spoke a word. I was then asked if I knew my nationality, but still, I never spoke. The police threatened to put me in an observation cell and was told that I would be speaking.

Govan police station is where terrorists are questioned in Scotland and I was taken there. Even though the police were trying to scare me into talking, I never opened my mouth, so they phoned my mum on my behalf, but still I never spoke.

I was then taken to another police station in Glasgow on Aitken Head Road. I never spoke the whole time, so I was kept on observation in a suicide cell. The next day, I was taken to Glasgow Sheriff Court where I was observed by the G4S 'janitors'.

I wasn't told what I was in for until I got to court, then I was given the summary with the charge I was facing. I was taken to the terrorist unit for a threatening phone call to my ex, who lived on the same street the terrorists lived on. Luckily, I was given bail.

While I was arrested and being driven to the police station, I heard the arresting officers talking about me committing an offence under the communications act. Then when I was taken into the Scottish Terrorist Unit, I thought it was because of a joke I cracked on Facebook. I'm talking about a picture that I posted of myself which is the front cover of this book. I said it was me who tried to blow up the Glasgow airport and I thought that's why I would be getting carted to court.

Chapter 102

I always kept in contact with Andy, in and out of prison, but he was mostly always inside. I wrote to him when I was in jail and when I was out, I visited him.

He served four years for possession of a gun and got out for a few short months, then was recalled to finish his six-year sentence, for a new minor offence. I never saw him when he was out, but he wrote to me when he was back in, asking me if he could come and live with me when he got back out. I went and visited him in Glenochil and I wanted Andy to stay with me when he got out. It would've been like the old times in Polmont.

When he got out, he moved to England. He phoned me and told me he was coming up, but I ended up in jail myself doing 12 months. I phoned him from jail and we wrote to each other.

Andy was avoiding police though because he was involved in a riot in HMP Glenochil (*before he was released*) and was carted to HMP Bow House in Kilmarnock. Then he was hiding out in England, before, he came back up to Greenock where he was arrested, but then bailed. He was expecting more years back in.

A few weeks later I saw a comment posted on his Facebook that read 'RIP'. I suddenly panicked and phoned the girl who was pregnant with his baby and asked what had happened. She told me that Andy had choked on his sick and died (*I cried*). Then this girl miscarried.

Andy died on his 28th birthday. The boy who found him dead was trying to wake him up to give him his birthday present but found him lying dead instead. I went to his funeral and met the boy who found him in his house. He told me that the priest asked Andy's sister, 'what was he good at'? And she said, "taking the blame for other people". He was a father at 16. I met his two children in Greenock when they were small and then I saw them at Andy's funeral. He was cremated in the Greenock Crematorium.

Andy used to text me every day (*even when he was in jail, he had a mobile*) and he would send me messages every single day in or out. He was with me in Kilmacolm the night 'D' got killed. 'D' was on his way to Kilmacolm as well, not to see me, but to camp along from my street.

I went to a Church meeting in Port Glasgow, where I met Andy's older brother and he told me that the autopsy showed that there were no drugs in his brother's system. So, I think it was the drink that killed him.

When Andy wrote to me from jail, asking if he could live with me when he got out, he told me he knew he would end up dead if he remained in Greenock. He told me that he didn't want this, but then he did die.

On Andy's first memorial, I flew from Glasgow airport to Belfast, to go to a rehab centre in Armagh but I left the next day. I got drunk and got the bus to Belfast where I met my dad's friend and he drove me to the dock where I got the boat back to Scotland. I would have been stranded in Stranraer, but I met two Irish boys who drove me to Glasgow, where I met my dad who took me back to my flat. I then went for drugs.

Andy was sent to Polmont for a year and a half when he was 18. He got out when he was 20 for a few months and was jailed for another 4 years. He was released, but very shortly recalled back to jail for another year.

After years of jail, he got out for a year, but before his release, he was involved in mobbing and rioting within a prison and was facing a further sentence of more years. I wish Andy hadn't got bailed for the rioting, or even that he had shot those two brothers in Greenock and was in jail doing 25 years to life. At least he'd still be alive.

The man gave Andy a shotgun and literally called the shots, asking him to fire the shots at these two brothers. Andy never pulled the trigger and then got six years jail for possession of the gun. Before this all happened, Andy was jailed for a week on remand for an attempted murder but walked. The man he stabbed was nearly killed as a favour, to the man who gave him the gun. Then Andy was meant to shoot the two men who got shot anyway (*by someone else*).

Andy always said that he would either die in Greenock or kill someone and told me he wanted neither. He went to jail at 18, came out at 20 only for a few months, then back in until he was 24. After this he was only out another few months, then back in until he was 26.

Going from an 18-year-old boy serving eight years in jail out of the last 10, Andy died outside on his 28th birthday, free from jail forever. Even after he was dead, his name was still appearing in the newspapers for rioting in Glenochil prison, but now he doesn't have to face anymore courts, judges or jail.

He grew up in jail and became a man inside prison. Then his life became being in jail for years and out to die on his birthday. That's the only thing that saved Andy from going back to jail. He died while on bail and took his last breath (*death*).

Chapter 103

After six months inside I came out of jail. I didn't drink or take any drugs for two months and I was at the gym every weekday, Monday to Friday. Then I drank again and couldn't stop. I ended up back on drugs as well.

I sat with a man called Kevin who lived in a flat around the corner at the shop. One day I saw Kevin and we walked over to the bank. While I was inside checking my balance, I looked outside and I saw Kevin standing talking and laughing away. When I came back outside, I saw for myself that he was having a full-blown conversation to himself. I asked him who he was talking to and quickly he snapped out of it and told me he was talking to me.

He introduced me to a man and I drank with him too. One day I was in the man's house sitting drinking my bottle of wine when the door went. It was the police.

It was the serious drugs squad wearing bullet proof vests. They had a search warrant for the house. I never spoke to the police and I was handcuffed and told to sit on a sofa while the house was turned over. There were four police all searching everywhere. I was then picked up and marched through to the bedroom where I was strip searched. They threatened to do me for obstruction, if I never spoke, but I never said a word for the whole hour.

They never found anything, so our handcuffs were taken off and the police left the house. The man who I met was previously a drug dealer and he moved to Kilmacolm and now the police tried to bust him (*but no drugs*). I only went around to drink my bottle of wine and I was detained while the CID turned the house over.

Apparently, this man was a gangster. He became a publican and people came to his pub to shoot him but shot his friend dead instead. Then people came and smashed their way through one of the windows of his house and murdered another one of his other friends with a hammer.

I introduced him to my dad who mentored him. He gave up drink and drugs and became a born- again Christian. You've heard of the goodfellas this is the God fella. He decided to follow the Lord and the Church did applaud, when he joined the God squad.

Chapter 104

K evin rented his flat as it was a private let but a letter was sent to his landlord and Kevin being Kevin opened the letter. It was a legal letter from Northern Rock. I didn't understand what he was talking about when he told me. I thought it was crack cocaine he was smoking and I knew he had lost it.

Kevin used to live in the grave digger's house in the Kilmacolm cemetery. I told him because of this, he'd lost the plot. He burst out laughing at my old joke and I looked into his eyes while he laughed. I could see the madness which I had seen in Carstairs, in him.

Every time I was with Kevin, he would tell me all about his fear of losing his flat. I felt sorry for him and I drank with him different days out of every week and he told me that I was his best friend. On that same day, he told me that the bailiffs were coming to repossess his house. He told me that he couldn't lose his flat and end up back in Greenock. He was in Greenock every day, but he didn't want to live there again.

He asked me if I would come and help him stand up to the bailiffs with the man, he had introduced me to, so we both did. And the three of us went to Kevin's door to challenge the bailiffs.

I met Kevin off the Greenock bus at the Cross and he went and bought me a half bottle of Buckfast. Kevin told me the bailiffs were coming at 10 o'clock and that's what time he bought me wine at. I drank half my bottle in one drink then we headed over to Kevin's house. As soon as we got near his building, we could hear the noise and commotion of his door being put in. We walked into Kevin's close where there was a team of men trying to batter his door down.

There were legal representatives who told Kevin that he wasn't allowed back into his flat. The man we were with pulled his mobile from his pocket and told them he was phoning the police. The bailiffs stalled for a few seconds then broke the door down, but because this man threatened to call the police, Kevin was told that he had one month before he had to leave the flat. The locks were changed and Kevin was given one of the new keys.

When the door was burst open, we all walked into the house to see that the flat was totally empty. The landlord had taken all the furniture, locked the door from the inside, then escaped through a hatch where a false loft had been built. The landlord was pocketing Kevin's housing benefit and the rent arrears were over £9000. We were all gob smacked.

Kevin bought me another half bottle and we walked up to his mother's house where we told her about the whole incident. I then walked with Kevin to the bus stop at the Cross and I got him on the bus. We had a good laugh as I saw him off.

Kevin told me he would see me the next day, but I never saw him. Sunday came and my dad went to Church, but I never went, I got drunk. I then went to see Kevin, but before I got to his house, I went into the corner shop to get a packet of cigarettes to take to share with him. While inside, the shop keeper told me that Kevin died.

I was shocked and I never took the smokes. I walked back out the shop door where I looked up at Kevin's house window.

Kevin was a Protestant and his job was a gardener to trade. He would go to Greenock where he cut a priest's garden. The same priest who did the service at Andy's funeral, spoke at Kevin's funeral too and a minister from Kilmacolm spoke as well in the Greenock Crematorium.

This minister was from the Church in Kilmacolm across the road from my house where we lived for over 25 years. Some years later the Kilmacolm Reverend ended up at court on fraud and embezzlement charges. He lost his position and job as minister, but miraculously walked free from court after a judge found him not guilty.

Kevin's brother who was in jail, also read out a poem that he had written. Years before I found his brother sleeping in the shed in my garden. I found a few people sleeping in it and two of them killed people.

Kevin's brother moved to England where he killed a man on Christmas day. He was dubbed, 'The Christmas Day Killer' (two *brothers - one killed a man and the other died himself*).

He couldn't handle losing his house in Kilmacolm and after months of torment he died in Greenock. Me and Kevin came to claim the same, we know his landlord is to blame.

Chapter 105

Years and years ago my granda's brother moved to New Zealand where he lived until he died. Before my granda was married he toured the world in the merchant navy. One of my granda's sisters had a baby before she was married and my granda's parents brought him up. My granda's nephew wasn't much younger than him and they classed each other as brothers.

He decided to follow in my granda's footsteps and joined the merchant navy where he sailed to New Zealand. While he was out celebrating his 21st birthday he missed his ship sailing away and he retired from the merchant navy and he stayed in New Zealand. He married a Maori girl and settled into their culture. His daughter married the leader of the Mighty Mongrel Mob which is a violent Maori gang who roam the country.

Actor and TV presenter Ross Kemp was out in New Zealand where he did a television programme on the gang. My second cousin who is married to the leader, never got mentioned, but I wrote to her and she wrote back.

My granda's nephew never came back to Scotland for over 50 years, then when he did, I met him at my mum's house. My granda was with us too and he seemed that close to his nephew who is my mum's cousin.

I have never been out to New Zealand to meet any of my second cousins. Although my sister, Bethany, flew over where my cousin and her husband picked her up at the airport in New Zealand.

My dad's ancestors were Irish travelers and I am Irish on both sides. My great granda was Irish. I am sallow skinned because I descended from Romani Gypsies and I do look like a foreign person.

I love caravans and I have been brought up going on holidays in them. When my mum and dad were first married, they lived in my granda's caravan in his garden. Then my dad got a house in Port Glasgow and stayed there until they moved back to Kilmacolm and started our family.

One Saturday, I went for a sauna in the Port Glasgow swimming pool with my dad and Gemma. In the steam room, I met a man who is my mum's full cousin. It's a small world after all!

After my granda became a widower, he went out to New Zealand to see all his family, where he met the leader of the Mob who he thought was a tribe man. My granda was happy to see all his family after my gran was dead. He didn't even realise this man was a gangster (*even though he had a mobster tattoo across his forehead*).

Chapter 106

I was sentenced to six months jail for threatening to kill the police. I was back in Low Moss. After a month I went back to Glasgow Sheriff Court and was jailed for another five months for a threatening phone call to my ex. I phoned her from jail and left a voicemail saying that I would see her in hell, so my sentence changed to 11 months.

I changed Gemma to my next of kin so that I could get an inter prison phone call and I got speaking to her twice, but then I threatened a screw and I was handcuffed and taken to the segregation unit. Two days later I went to the orderly room in front of the governor. I was found guilty and sentenced to three days in the cells. I had already done two. I was also told that I was getting moved to Barlinnie after my time in solitary.

Tuesday came and I was taken to Barlinnie and I was pleased. I had six weeks to go until I was out and I liked Barlinnie, not Low Moss now. It wasn't bad when it first opened, but it became slow moss because it went slow and did my head in. I was put in D-Hall first night - centre. Then the next day I was moved over to B-Hall. I was in B-Hall for two weeks, then I was moved over to D-Hall for a month and got back into the gym. I had been in for over five months and I was looking forward to getting out. The jail kept me sober and put me in a bubble, but every time I came out, the bubble burst and I ended up burst.

I used to weigh nine stone but the medication I'm prescribed makes me hungry with a bottomless pit appetite. I went over-weight and I ended up at 16 stone, but then I would go back on drugs and lose weight again. Then when I was inside prison, I would lift weights and get toned. I wasn't fat, I wasn't skinny, I was in Barlinnie.

Chapter 107

Before I got out, Paddy was murdered. He was stabbed five times and took a cardiac arrest and died. You live by the sword, you die by the sword and Paddy lived that way. He was no stranger to being in jail or attempted murders.

He walked for different attempted murders at the High Court and he walked for serious assaults at the Sheriff Court as well (*all knife attacks*). He was never found not guilty, always not proven, which means they knew he done it, but couldn't prove it.

Every jail I was in, I was in with Paddy. I saw him everywhere (*Gateside*, *Polmont*, *Barlinnie* and *Low Moss*). I only ever saw him once on the outside. With my dad, we were in the Struthers cafe-teria in Greenock, getting some soup. After I finished my bowl, I looked out the window and saw Paddy walking through the street. I walked out quickly and met him. I shook his hand and we had a chat.

At that time my dad was cited as a member of the jury for a crim-inal case. Paddy's brother was going to trial for a stabbing and my dad had been cited as a juror. My dad told Paddy that he wouldn't go ahead with it. My dad told the system that he knew the boy, so he was put off the juror's list.

My mum was called to be a juror twice, but she wrote two letters trying to get herself off with it. The first letter was when I was in the hospital after I was nearly killed. The second time she got off with it because she told them she was a nurse who worked with the public.

I was still in jail at the time of Paddy's funeral, but my mum went on my behalf. In the Greenock Crematorium, a poem was read out in memory of Paddy which he had written in jail about him dying. His brother later told me that this poem had been published.

Me and Paddy never did any big jail sentences. Only 30 months here and 16 months there, but in the end Paddy's last sentence was three years for a possession of a knife in jail. He tried to hang himself in there and was taken to hospital where he attacked the prison guard. He survived and got out.

On Tuesday, 27th August 2013, Paddy posted a comment on Facebook stating that he was leaving his hometown, but three days later in the early hours of Friday 30th August, he was killed. If he had left Greenock when he said, he shouldn't be dead.

I'm not surprised that Paddy got killed. I always thought this would happen to him, or, that he would kill someone else at some point. He was very vicious, but in the end, he was killed for his own violent actions. He brought it upon himself, but he wasn't really the victim. Someone else was.

On the night he died, Paddy robbed a 20-year-old man at knife point taking his iPhone from him. The victim then went home and told his dad who along with his brothers went out armed with knives looking for Paddy. The man traced him with an app on his own iPhone. When he found his son's mugger, he confronted him. Paddy then gouged the man's eye out with the knife he had, while the man's sons stabbed Paddy to death.

The father took the blame and his three sons went free while he went to jail for six years with only one eye. He might have lost an eye (*and went to jail on his own*), but at least he got his son's iPhone.

Chapter 108

G etting out of prison is an incredible feeling, but obviously someone has to go to jail to be able to experience this wonderful experience and who wants to go to jail? No one (*except someone like me*).

For years my life was a misery, on and off drugs. Mostly always on. The only time I was happy was when I was in jail. When I got out of prison, I was a mess on drink and drugs. The alcohol turned me into a totally different person. I'm much nicer to be around when I'm sober. I was horrible to my friends and family. Now all I have is my family. The cannabis that I was smoking fried my head and I watched violence on the television all the time. I was out to make a reputation for myself and I lived in this too long. Even after I stopped carrying knives, I still threatened people with violence. I lived in nostalgia and I was consumed by anger for years. I was full of resentment and I was bitter inside.

I was never tough in any way, but for years I wasn't happy, unless I was in a violent place. That's why I moved to Greenock and then got myself jailed. The jail kept me alive, happy and also happy to be alive, but I can't go back to jail now. So, I had to find happiness on the outside (*without drugs*). My wife and my son do make me happy, but living your life in addiction, the temptation is always there. The bible says *resist and the devil will flee*.

I have been an addict for over half my life and I know that I will always think about drugs until the day I die, but that doesn't mean I have to take them.

Every year I would come off drink and drugs for Christmas and every new year's resolution for years was for me to stay clean, but I failed every year, until now. I love Christmas time, getting presents and all the lovely food. Ironic that the customary meal is cooked turkey and every year I had to do a cold turkey.

When you get addicted to drugs, they will never satisfy you, but by that point you are trapped in your addiction. Trying to satisfy your habit is like chasing a rainbow, you will never get the pot of gold. I should know, I was taking drugs since I was 12 years old (*trust what I have told*).

Chapter 109

One night, Wilky came through to my flat in Bridge of Weir to stay for a couple of nights. That night we spoke about Carstairs and some of their patients.

It didn't take long before we spoke about the chunky chicken man. Wilky had written a song about him. He played the song on his phone and we chatted about the lunatic's efforts to get a Michael Jackson suit. That night I went to my bed and fell asleep, leaving Wilky in the living room on the couch. At five o'clock in the morning, my phone rang and I was wakened. It was my dad who told me that the police were at my family door looking for 'Chunky' because he had done a runner from a shopping trip.

The police woke my dad up out of his sleep because 'Chunky' had phoned me from Carstairs, but they never came over to my own flat to search the place. The searching officers told my dad that the missing mental patient wasn't dangerous, but while he was in Carstairs, he was apparently too dangerous to be allowed to use a razor blade, so the nurses shaved him instead, cutting his face. Then he tried to sue the State Hospital but failed because he was a high-profile criminal lunatic.

I went into the living room, woke Wilky up and told him what was happening and we couldn't believe it. We were talking about this specific patient only a few hours before.

Later that same day, Wilky's mobile rang and it was the police looking for the escaped patient because Wilky was in contact with him as well. Wilky had just recently changed his mobile phone number, but the police had somehow got his new number.

After a few hours on the run 'Chunky' surrendered and handed himself into a local police station. Headlines in the newspapers were, 'Dangerous Psychiatric Patient Who Went on The Run Hands Himself in to Police'. The police told my dad that he wasn't dangerous. Well, why were they at my family home at five o'clock in the morning?

Me and Wilky couldn't believe it, that we were both together when all this happened, but at least we can say that we know Michael Jackson's number one fan (*the chunky chicken man*).

Chapter 110

Gemma was out on a home leave and we were together every day. She was staying at her cousin's house in Saltcoats, then we went to her mother's home in Glasgow. Then we went to my flat in Bridge of Weir. That night Gemma looked out my window and told me that she could see a helicopter flying above while shining their torch through my living room window.

It was the police helicopter and it was out circulating the area because there had been a murder a mile away, in Bridge of Weir.

A man was camping near the river and was bashed about the head with a blunt object and was found murdered in the Locher water. His friend was found hurt as well and was left with leg injuries. I saw him staggering around the village with crutches and then a stick during his recovery, but then eight months after the murder, the man was arrested and charged with the killing. He went to prison on remand for only a few weeks, then was freed from jail on bail for nearly a year. He went to trial, was found guilty and jailed for life. He got 17 years for his efforts.

The killer walked into the Glasgow High Court that morning, was found guilty and sentenced to life later that day. He previously had it in for me, because I beat his stepson up for kicking my door in. One night, months before the murder happened, the would-be killer was hiding in my close waiting for me, but my neighbour caught him and he ran away.

The police came to my door to talk to me about the murder, but I just ignored them. They came back four times (*that I know of*) and they put a police card through my door. The police even went over to Kilmacolm to my family home looking for me. I wasn't a suspect. They had a questionnaire sheet and were knocking everyone's door in my scheme. I knew they wouldn't come through my door with a questionnaire, but finally I answered and spoke to them through my locked grill gate. I said, "No" to every single question, except one. I told them that I was in my flat when the murder happened. What I didn't tell them was that my alibi was a known murderer.

Gemma never murdered anyone. She was the victim of a miscarriage of justice! Her mum stabbed a man through the heart (*killing him*) and then along with her stepdad, blamed Gemma for the murder. Gemma's mum got jailed for life too, although she only got a 10 years tariff while poor Gemma was jailed for 12 years to life. They became the first mother and daughter in Scotland to get jailed together for life for murder.

Before they got jailed, Gemma's aunt also murdered a man and was jailed for life too. She ended up in Carstairs from where she was sent back to jail. She hung herself and then died in hospital.

When Gemma was heavily pregnant, I moved to a bigger house in Bridge of Weir. Within a year, my old downstairs neighbour was gunned down on Halloween. He survived and his shooter got 12 years for his efforts.

My old neighbour opened an ice cream shop in Bridge of Weir called Tasty Treats and I'm sure he must have admitted defeat when he got shot with a shotgun on Halloween (*trick or treat*).

Chapter 111

When I moved into my first flat in Bridge of Weir, I met one of my neighbour's who lived across the street from me. Ronnie kept lurchers and he took them out hunting and he went fishing as well.

I went to jail for six months and I thought about getting a lurcher. Then, I came out and I wanted one but after eight months, I was back in jail before I managed to buy this kind of dog. When I came out, I was determined to get a hunting dog, but I decided not to keep it in my house so I asked Ronnie if he would keep it for me and he told me he would.

Ronnie didn't have a dog at this time. He hadn't had one for a while. Then one morning I went on 'Gumtree dogs Scotland' and I saw that there was a lurcher for sale in Blantyre, Glasgow. As soon as I read that the dog was coming from Blantyre, I wanted the pup because the murder that Gemma got jailed for, happened in Blantyre, so to me it was a sign, or, maybe just a coincidence.

I asked Ronnie what the best hunting dog was to get and he told me to get a collie, whippet, greyhound and that's the one that was for sale. So, acting on impulse, I phoned Ronnie at seven o'clock in the morning and told him that I was going to buy it. I asked a man to take me to get the dog, but he got arrested for driving offences. My mum drove us through to Blantyre, where we met two men at Lidl's supermarket. I paid £250 for the 11-week-old bitch and I wanted to call her Gypsy. The guy who sold her told me that her name was in fact already Gypsy.

I was chuffed with the dog and so was Ronnie. I phoned Wilky and he came through and stayed with me for the night. My sister Bethany was over as well with the pup, but Ronnie was wrecked. The first night we got Gypsy, he was full of valium.

Round about the same time I moved to Bridge of Weir, Ronnie became a father and he had a daughter. He wasn't together with his daughter's mother, but Ronnie was a good dad. His ex-didn't think so and she wouldn't let him see his own daughter.

He fought a social work battle and was getting supervised visits in the Greenock Social Work Department. My dad ran Ronnie to the Greenock Court for a hearing.

Meanwhile Gypsy was a disaster. Ronnie couldn't control her, he was taking as much valium as he could get, so we couldn't get the puppy toilet trained. She would do the toilet everywhere. I gave him a cage to keep Gypsy in, but he would let the dog out and it would do the toilet on his living room carpet while Ronnie lay sparkled on the couch.

I had stopped taking valium, but I smoked hash with Ronnie and we took cocaine. Ronnie couldn't get it together for Gypsy and for the good of the dog, I had to take her from him and give her to someone else.

Ronnie used to catch rabbits, foxes and deer with his previous lurchers. He ate rabbit and went fishing as well. He told me he sold venison to the butchers. Ronnie took my brother in law fishing for an hour and they caught five fish.

He'd never been to jail, but he'd been caught growing marijuana plants a few times and a couple of people asked me if I would grow a yield in my flat. I couldn't because I am with Gemma who is on life licence, but I set Ronnie up to grow for a boy. So, we got all the equipment and started a cannabis factory, (*Or so we thought*).

The plants grew but there were no buds, so Ronnie cut them down. He started another crop, again, but he was wrecked for days and the plants became a failed cannabis farm. Then on my wedding day Ronnie took a major heart attack.

Ronnie had asked me if he could come to my wedding and I told him that he could, but it was family only, because of our fear of media coverage. It was a small wedding and very quickly over with. Gemma had to go back to jail at tea-time that night.

Ronnie died. The major heart attack was fatal. I sat with him every single day as well. He would come over to mine first thing in the morning. He never locked his front door, so you just walk into his living room, where he lay on his couch, day in, day out, watching a broken telly. Ronnie watched a broken television for about two years. Then he broke his broken telly. Ronnie was broken.

He never got to see his daughter anymore and then took a fatal heart attack on the same day that I got married. Then he died a few days later on my dad's birthday. If I did invite Ronnie, then he would maybe have taken the heart attack at my wedding, or, he might have passed out in my flat some other time.

On my wedding night, my family ended up at my sister's house in Port Glasgow and then my mum drove us home to Kilmacolm with my niece in the back of the car. On our way home, my mum hit a deer in Port Glasgow, but the deer ran away. Luckily, we never came off the road.

I gave up on trying to hunt animals and I bought my son two pet rabbits. Then one of them escaped out of the hutch early one morning. When I found out she was gone, I thought surely that she would be dead. Then my downstairs neighbour came to our door that night telling us that one of our other neighbour's had found the rabbit. When we contacted them, they told us someone else had our pet. In the end up a woman we knew brought our rabbit home. I was certain that the rabbit would be dead so, I never even prayed that we would get her back, but a Christian blessed us with my son's pet rabbit.

I bought Gypsy to hunt rabbits, foxes and deer and with my own eyes, I have seen her chase all these animals, but she has never killed anything, although, while sitting in the back of her new owner's car, he hit a deer. Ironic that Gypsy can't catch anything and then is in a smash up with a deer! I don't think the deer died either (*oh dear*). Gypsy was taken away from Bridge of Weir which was clear.

Chapter 112

When I got Gemma pregnant, I gave up my flat in Church Road, but I was given another (*bigger*) house in Bridge of Weir. When Ronnie died, I left my old flat after a number of weeks, then a few weeks later I became a dad. I moved over to my new house which was in the same building that Ronnie took his heart attack in.

My new neighbour, Coggie, was a 47-year-old man, who rented the spare-room in his flat to a 19-year-old boy. When I was getting my new house decorated, we could smell burning coming from his house. Then I looked out my living room window and I could see two fire engines outside my building. I heard banging and shouting in the close, so I went out my front door to see what all the commotion was.

It was firemen kicking my neighbour's front door, trying to get through it, but they failed. The smoke alarm from his flat was screeching. Then low and behold Coggie opens his door with no shoes on, wearing a skip hat. He had burnt his dinner.

He had been making a meal and fell asleep full of valium and now all this commotion. I thought for a minute he was dead just like Ronnie. After all Ronnie took a fatal heart attack in this same house and was carried to a hospital where he died. This could have easily been a house fire in my neighbour's flat, in the same building, me and Gemma were to live in.

Every day for years, Coggie was on drugs and the life he was living was dire, but surely God could take away this terrible desire and we knew that we would get on with him, like a house on fire.

Chapter 113

The 19-year-old boy that Coggie had staying with him sold drugs and Coggie's lodger fed his habit on a daily basis. One day me and Gemma were walking down our stairs when she found a bag with quite a lot of cocaine and some marijuana in it. I weighed the stash in my house with the scales that I had and found out that there were 160 grams of cocaine and a few ounces of weed. We then lied and told the 19-year-old that we never found his drugs. He later told me that he knew it was me all along.

My neighbour dealer was selling drugs from right under my nose and he let me run up a £1000 debt within about a fortnight. I was addicted to cocaine, then we found his stash, which kept my habit going.

I was waking up in the morning and sniffing big lines first thing for five days, but then I flushed the last 60 grams down the toilet because I was sick of my addiction. I know that I should have posted the remaining stash through my neighbour's door, but I never. Instead I flushed it down the toilet pan. I did feel bad for bumping the boy's drugs, but it's a big bad world and I think I taught him a valuable lesson. Don't trust anyone, especially not when an amount of drugs like that is involved.

It's his own fault anyway. I mean who would throw 160 grams of cocaine down in a building for anyone to find? Me and my wife found it and hammered basically 100 grams in under a week. The young boy was the flavour of the month when he had gear, but when he ran out of drugs he ran out of friends.

There was a guy called Heaney who lived parallel to our building. We lived on Mimosa Road and Heaney lived on Houston Road. One night, Heaney came to Coggie's house where he sat with me and my younger neighbour. Coggie's cooker wasn't working properly and the boy he had staying with him had a steak pie from Marks and Spencer's, so he asked if he could make it in my flat. After we made it and ate it, we went back down to Coggie's, where we sat until about midnight when I left and went back up the stairs to my own flat. Heaney was in Coggie's when I left. Shortly after I left, Coggie went to his bed then the 19-year-old boy went to his bed as well in the other room. Heaney followed my younger neighbour into his room where he lay on the carpet.

The next day, I walked down the stairs to Coggie's flat and his front door was unlocked, so I walked in and I saw a big police-man standing in the hall right at the doorway of my 19 year-old neighbour's bedroom. The policeman told me to leave, so I left. I thought it was a drug's bust. I walked out of our building and I passed a big police van parked outside. I went to the shops and then came back to my flat. Coggie phoned me and told me that Heaney had passed away. He was dead in the same house that

Ronnie had took his fatal heart attack in. How did he die? We don't actually know. The 19-year-old boy thought that he was sleeping. He was sleeping, then he died in his sleep.

The night before he died, Heaney was laughing away to himself in a wee world of his own. I knew he was telling himself jokes. After I left Coggie's house, he followed my younger neighbour into his room and died on the carpet.

The police left poor Heaney's body on the carpet for 10 hours. It was suspicious circumstances after all. Ronnie too, a heart attack in the same house, only a year before. Ronnie wasn't officially dead for another five days. The hospital kept him alive on a life support machine, but he was taking seizures when doctors tried to revive him. This was now the second body to be carried out of Coggie's.

Coggie and the 19-year-old boy were under house arrest - they weren't allowed out the house. The police let me go to local shop and buy them cigarettes and juice, but I wasn't even allowed inside the house. I had to hand the stuff to the police. Heaney told me he couldn't live another 30 years like the way he was living, but he only lasted another year.

After 10 months my younger neighbour left my building and went back to live in his family home. He told everyone he ended up a patient in a mental hospital, but this boy was a compulsive liar. The lies constantly spilled out his mouth. Maybe he was a mental patient? He couldn't handle the life he led, or the thoughts in his head, because Heaney was dead, he was having nightmares in his bed (*or so he said*).

Chapter 114

C oggie didn't believe in God, he was basically an atheist. So, I told him that I could prove to him that God does exist and he took me up on my offer. I took him with me to one of my dad's meetings. My dad prayed for Coggie and suddenly, he felt the power of God coming through him. After my dad stopped praying,

Coggie asked me what had just happened and I told him that it was the power of God that he could feel.

Coggie told me that the feeling he felt was better than any drug he'd ever taken. He became faithful and came to all my dad's meetings and I convinced him to go to a Christian rehab so that he could get off drugs. He went and gave his life to God and is now a born-again Christian.

Coggie was a Protestant who didn't believe in God but before he went to rehab, I went downstairs into his house to sit with him and I put on Magic radio station. While we were listening to it, Coggie told me that he was a Christian now and that he wasn't a Protestant anymore. Instantly, the Tina Turner song '*Simply the Best*' came on the radio station. Coggie couldn't believe it, because this song as most of us know has been adopted by Glasgow Rangers which is a Protestant football team. It just shows you that God has a sense of humour and isn't just a religious rumour.

Chapter 115

Because of the life I chose (*drugs and jail*) I have lived through and experienced quite a lot of death at such a young age, but all these deaths are not coincidental. God was in them all.

Kevin's memorial is the 1st of March. A week later (8th March), it's Paul's memorial and also Blaney's birthday. Paul died on Blaney's birthday. Andy died on his own birthday and Yogi died on Halloween. Dunga's friend, was buried in Kilmacolm and his funeral was held in Saint Francis of Assisi chapel in Port Glasgow. Lynchy was cremated in Greenock and his ashes were scattered in the grounds of St Francis's. Yogi and Blaney are buried right behind each other in the Kilbarchan cemetery. Their gravestones are back to back. They never even knew each other, they met through me.

These people didn't all know each other, but the ones who did, fought each other. Ronnie stabbed Paul and Yogi punched Blaney and with another boy they bit a chunk out of Ronnie's ear. The council offered the house that Paul was to die in. Yogi died on Halloween, then the boy who bit Ronnie's ear died too (*sometime later*). Then Ronnie took a major heart attack on my wedding day in a house which was my neighbour's and then he died on my dad's birthday. Heaney died in the same house.

All these people that I bonded with have departed and their memories are left intertwined through me. I took drugs with most of them and no matter how close they were to me, their deaths had some kind of impact on me. RIP. I don't know who of you I will see again, but to those I will, I will see you soon.

I went to the Glasgow Prophetic Centre where two young Christians prophesied over me. They told me that when the Holy Spirit comes into me, no high on this earth can beat that. They were right. The prophets also told me that I have gifting like them. I didn't have to pay any money for the prophetic reading. The gospel is free, although I didn't know, they were going to make a prophet out of me.

Chapter 116

One day my dad came and told me that he'd heard Eggy was missing. In the next few days articles started appearing in the newspapers, stating him as a missing person. He was prescribed methadone, but he never went to the chemist to get his daily dose and he also never lifted his benefit from the bank either. As the days went on, I knew that he was dead.

After about a week of being missing the police announced that they'd found Eggy's body. Then articles started appearing in the newspapers, stating that his remains were discovered. Within a few hours the newspaper stories printed that Eggy was dismembered. By the next day, there were stories printed in all the countries newspapers that Eggy's torso was found but his head wasn't.

A 46-year-old man was charged with murdering Eggy with a machete and chopping his body up and leaving his torso near the outside bins stuffed in a suitcase. The murderer was remanded in custody and sent to jail for months until trial, where he was found guilty and jailed for life.

This man who murdered Eggy, previously killed his own father. Years ago, when I was in Carstairs I read it in the newspaper, that he stabbed his father to death with a sword in Kilbarchan, but because his dad abused his family, the killer was only given five years for culpable homicide.

What was left of Eggy's corpse was found in Gallowhill in Paisley where my sister used to live. She had sold her flat when the murder happened and moved to Port Glasgow, where there was another murder on her new street. My sister's house in Port Glasgow was basically a stone throw away from Greenock. The murder that happened on her street was a stone throw away as well.

The Port Glasgow killer pled not guilty and walked free by grounds of self defence. Eggy's murderer pled self defence too, but then was found guilty of mutilating Eggy and was sentenced to a minimum of 26 years in jail, but then he appealed the length of his sentence and had his tariff cut down by four years bringing his punishment part to 22 years. Whatever the killer's sentence, he might never get out. When jailing him for his barbaric deed, the judge told him he might never be freed. I'm sure his victim's family agreed.

Chapter 117

I never asked to be an alcoholic, but I suppose no one does. I just loved wine that much, I drank it every day, not giving it a moment's thought. Now I think about it a lot, because I know it will kill me and I have so much to live for.

Boredom is a killer and I drank for something to do in my spare time. It was killing me, not the boredom (*the wine*).

I loved Buckfast and I chose to drink it every day, but when I tried to stop, I found it really hard. The cravings were terrible and once the cravings left me the boredom set in. Back to the boredom. Drugs are not the answer. It's death by instalments.

I was searching for a high all my life and I took more or less every drug that I could get my hands on, but God had his hand on me. I have known of God all my life and after everything I've been through, my faith is what keeps me strong.

Deep down inside me, I longed to be free from addiction for years, but my thoughts were to take drugs again on most days. In my heart I wanted freedom from addiction but in my head, I wanted drugs and more drugs. I will be an addict until the day I die. Only when I pass away, will I be free from this horrible curse, which is self-inflicted.

So, to anyone who loves drink and drugs the way I did, well you don't want to go through what I've been through, unless you think it's worth it.

I've been in and out of institutions for 19 years. Also, drinking and taking drugs for all that time as well. Because of the life I lived, obviously, I didn't care if I went to jail, but a lot of the time, I got myself jailed on purpose. I know to most people the jail is horrible, but I enjoyed it mostly and it kept me alive.

After becoming addicted, the drugs didn't make me happy, instead, they made me very unhappy. I'm at my happiest when I am straight and only in the jail could I remain clean as there's no shops selling Buckfast inside prison!

I used to get paid fortnightly until I wrote a letter to the benefits agency telling them that I couldn't manage my money at a fortnightly rate. So, my money was changed to weekly payments, but then I started taking heroin every week. When I got my money, I would smoke heroin. I was a 'giro junkie'.

It says in the Bible *(and in Trainspotting)*, "Choose Life" and I did choose heroin every Tuesday.

I called it a 'Tuesday charge' but really, it was a choose day charge because I would burn away every pay day *(which was a Tuesday)*.

Chapter 118

When my son was born there were complications and it was a horrendous labour for my wife. Over 30 hours it lasted and, in the end, it was a forceps delivery. The nurses who were in charge of my son's birth, brought in the resuscitation trolley because our baby got stuck and his heart rate got low, but then my son came out fine, after all the pain. He was kept in hospital for two months because he was lactose intolerant and had other problems.

I was at the hospital every day in Wishaw and I had been sober nearly five months, but I could see my son was suffering so I drank again. When my baby came out of the hospital it all caught up with me and I ended up back on drink and drugs (*every day*), so I got myself arrested one Friday night for a breach of the peace.

I lay in the cell in the Greenock police station all weekend, broken. At court on Monday my lawyer told me that he would get me out, but I refused bail and asked for the jail, but because I hadn't committed a crime in four years, the judge wouldn't give me a custodial sentence, but remanded me for three weeks for social enquiry reports. So, I got my wish and I was jailed. I was sent to HMP Gateside in Greenock.

This jail broke me. I couldn't stop thinking about getting out. Every day I prayed that when I went back to court, I would get bailed.

I read my Bible every day (*daily readings*), but none of what I read for three weeks meant anything to me. Then on the morning before court, I read my new testament Bible and the words I read were, *on their release, Peter and John went back to their own people and reported all that the chief priests had said to them.* On that very day, the judge did release me. So, I believe that God spoke to me that morning through his Word.

I used to love being in jail, so I broke the law. Every day dragged in. It was as slow as a weekend in Wishaw.

Chapter 119

As I told you before, I was born on my granda's birthday. The day he turned 51, I was born. The last time I was in jail I wrote to my granda. He never wrote back, but he thought that I had gone religious because of what I wrote in my letter. I was turning 32 and my granda was turning 83, so I asked him to make his peace with God. I told him that Jesus died for him and that whoever believes in Him will go to Heaven and that my gran was up there waiting on him.

I got out of jail a week before our birthday and we celebrated our birthdays together, but exactly a month later my granda died. He took a fatal heart attack and died in his bedroom, where my gran had died 20 years before, in the same room.

My sister Natalie, who found my gran dead in her bed, hadn't went up the stairs in 20 years, but she went up at this time to see my granda's body.

Along with my brother and two sisters we all went to the funeral parlour in Greenock to see my granda's body. I loved him very much and I cried deeply for him.

My dad told me that it was God who prompted me to write that letter from jail and I believe it was. Just after he died, I found out that my granda went to Church with Grace and also that he was reading Christian books. So, I do believe in my heart that my granda did make his peace with God and made it to Heaven. He is up there now with my gran.

Along with my brother, sisters, dad and uncle, we all carried my granda's coffin in and out of the Old Kirk in Kilmacolm. Then we all took a cord lowering him down into his grave.

My granda sold his caravan a year before he died. He then went on holiday to Millport because he was too old to travel far. He came back his holiday on the Friday and then he died on the Sunday.

My mum and dad took my baby over on the ferry to meet my granda and Grace on their holiday. One of the last times my granda phoned my mum, was to tell her that I was in the Greenock Telegraph newspaper, because I was in jail.

It's very sad to lose my granda as he loved his family very much. He didn't like football and didn't support a team. If ever asked what team he supported, he said none. He told people he supported his family because they support him.

Because me and my brother became fathers my granda became a Great Grandfather and he really was a great granda. He loved my son and my niece too and another sad fact is that they just started their lives as he ended his.

Grace decided that my granda was to get buried in with my gran in the Kilmacolm Cemetery because that's what he would have wanted, which was another lovely thing for her to do. My gran and granda are buried together now and they are back together in the next life as well.

I got booked up for a tattoo on my granda's first memorial and because my granda was in the merchant navy, my two sisters got anchor tattoos. I decided to get an anchor-cross to symbolise my granda's career and the fact I believe he is in Heaven.

Also, on the first anniversary of my granda's death his dog died. It wasn't a sudden death like my granda's. Grace had to get their dog put down.

Grace got my dad to go to the vet and pick up the dog's ashes. She told us she was going to scatter them over my granda's grave. My granda had diabetes then the dog became diabetic too.

After my granda was dead a couple of years, I went to the doctor's in Houston where I had my urine screened. The doctor then told me that I had sugar in my sample. I then had to get my blood taken. My dad drove me to the surgery that morning, but beforehand I went into the local kiosk and bought two bottles of Irn Bru. When I got into my dad's car, he had already got two bottles, so we ended up with four bottles of Irn Bru.

I normally drank a bottle first thing in the morning, but I didn't this time because I knew the doctor would want to check my urine. I knew I might be diabetic too and I was surrounded by Irn Bru.

The day I got diagnosed with diabetes, I walked into the doctor's office carrying a bottle of Diet Coca Cola. As soon as the doctor saw what I had in my hand, he told me that I needed diet juice now. I knew at that point I had diabetes and I had to stop taking sugar like other diabetic folk. I loved Cola but I had to switch to Diet Coke (*no joke*).

Chapter 120

My dad has a friend who lives over in Northern Ireland. This man was involved in the Protestant Paramilitaries back in the 70s but is now a Christian. Me and my dad have been over to Belfast a few different times to stay with our friend. He takes us round all the murals and I love seeing them all.

I was born in Scotland, but I am Irish on both sides. My mum's granda was from Ballymena. I'm Romani descent; my dad's forefathers were Irish travelers. I am sallow skinned because of my Romani blood, but we don't know what actual country our ancestors came from.

In Ireland, the hatred between Protestants and Catholics has calmed down now but has always been an ongoing issue. There is a wall built in Belfast to separate the Protestants on the Shankill Road and the Catholics on Falls Road.

The wall is called the peace-line and when I was 14 me and my dad went over to Belfast on the boat and we were both sick as dogs on the Sea Cat. I wrote my name on the peace-line with a bucket of paint and a paint brush. As time went by my mention got painted over so when I was 32, we went back over and I spray painted my name on it this time.

Me and my dad flew over to Belfast in February 2018 and while we were over there a snowstorm came from Russia and we were stranded in Belfast for an extra two days because of the weather.

I was drinking again before we went, but I detoxed myself while we were away and my wife Gemma said that it was God who stranded me in Northern Ireland, so that I could stay sober for longer and maybe she was right.

I used to support Celtic, but I gave up following football because I didn't like the fact that people who support this team are classed as Catholics. One of my granda's sisters converted to Catholicism in order to marry her husband of the same religion.

Years ago, before I was born my gran told my mum not to bring a Catholic boy to her house. Then my dad came to their door with a Celtic top on with a bag of alcohol. My gran wasn't happy. I love God and I'm very proud of my Protestant heritage. My dad got drink from the shop and then went to my gran's wearing a Celtic top.

Chapter 124

Taking drugs is what my generation did. Every drug I took got offered to me by someone else. I know I could have said no, but I just wanted to fit in. I wanted to be normal and growing up, illegal chemicals were the norm.

Out of all the drugs I took, alcohol was the hardest one to beat. I have craved cannabis, cocaine, Buckfast and heroin. I always thought that I was on top of smack and that it would never get me, but it did. I thought I was alright because I never injected and I wasn't on methadone, but I was constantly at rock bottom.

If I drink, I will need drugs. I drank every morning, smoked hash every day, took cocaine and heroin when I got money. Then I moved on to crack. Putting aside alcoholism, I am definitely a drug addict. I craved Buckfast which although it's an alcoholic drink, it's also a drug and alcohol is the worst drug! Although most people don't know it.

In Scotland as soon as you turn 18 years old you have a legal right to kill yourself with alcohol and I was drinking myself to death.

For years I needed drugs every day and alcohol is the most available drug. I lived at the Kilmacolm Cross, where the shops were right at my doorstep. At first drink and drugs made me happy, but then they got a right grip of me and I didn't like them anymore. To be truthful, I hated them. I didn't love it at all anymore and I hated being trapped in addiction and I was sick of it.

I was in hospital three times because of alcohol. I couldn't stop being sick and I was sick of being sick. After I came out of hospital the last time, more or less every drink I took made me vomit. It was like I was bulimic with wine. I was making myself throw up every day. Day in day out every time I drank. I couldn't keep the alcohol down in my stomach and I was sick and tired of it. I knew I was going to die. It's like I was terminally ill with the drink. I was slowly but surely committing suicide.

For a long time, I had a death wish but I never managed to kill myself, although I was broken inside. Hurt people, hurt people and I was living my life in misery through addiction. My mental health was like mental agony. I have been prescribed anti-depressants ever since I was 13 but I self-medicated with drink and drugs to take my pain away.

I'm a lazy person, but I know that I need to keep busy and some people say that I should find an interest. It is sad that my hobby will kill me but at least I know it will, but this is all I've done in my life. Taking drugs and drinking was what I have done. I loved it and I was a stoner at 14 and I loved a drink. Then at 17, I had a drink problem and I never even knew it. I first tried drinking cider, wine and beer in Bridge of Weir and all these years later I'm still here.

Chapter 122

I was drunk one day and I met Blaney's granda. He invited me to alcoholics anonymous. I knew I was an alcoholic, so I started going to the AA. I still got drunk most days, but I was wanting to fight to get sober. This has been my life since I was 22, trying to battle an addiction.

At the AA, I learned about finding a 'Higher Power', to get me sober and at once I knew that they were talking about God. Alcoholism is an illness which is three-fold in nature (*physical, mental and spiritual*). So being alcoholic, I should stay away from the first drink at all costs. I also learned that alcoholism is insanity and when I was a teenager, I loved all that madness. Buckfast was my favourite drug. Even though ecstasy and cocaine felt better, tonic wine was my drug of choice but really, I didn't have much of a choice. When I took that first drink, I wouldn't be able to stop. I started a compulsion that becomes a mental obsession, where I end up with the phenomenon of craving. I would crave fortified wine every day and when I drank, I would want illegal substances to enhance the pleasure and for maximum effect.

I'm not trying to glorify drugs in any way. The misery of addiction was more powerful than the good times. For a long time, I wanted to die. I didn't enjoy the taste of any alcohol that I drank. I drank to get drunk, ever since I was 13 years old. I got drunk for 20 years and I was an addict at 15, then jailed at 17. I still used drugs inside prison, but not nearly as much as I did on the outside. However, I did stop drinking. When I was 22, I realised that I was an alcoholic and I was fighting to get sober ever since.

I had never taken heroin or cocaine before I got locked up. I tried these class A drugs while I was inside Carstairs and Polmont. Then, after coming out I got addicted to them years later. One day, I prayed to God to show me a sign to help me on my Christian journey. Then I walked down to the shops where I met a man and woman from the AA. Shortly after this Gemma phoned me from jail and told me that she wanted to become a Christian. So that was the sign that I prayed for. I never thought for a minute that the sign was the couple from AA that I met. God touched Gemma's heart in jail and that was my prayer answered.

When I came out of jail after my last sentence, I drank within a week. The next day I tried to fight the addiction and stay sober. I went to a house where a neighbour's dog bit me. The dog's owner then gave me £40 because his dog ripped my trousers. I went and bought wine and hash and spoke about the devil dog who put me on it!

My life was drinking wine and taking drugs every day, in and out of jail for years. I knew that I had to change, or I would end up dead. My lifestyle would become my death, but I couldn't get sober on my own will power. I had to use my Higher Power.

Before I got addicted, I loved all these chemicals, but they're not worth dying for. Although when I do go to Heaven that will be my most incredible experience. I can't wait to go over the rainbow.

Chapter 123

G emma has a bad back and in jail she was prescribed pregabalin for her pain. When she came out after 12 years in jail, she gave birth to my son, two months later. Not long after this, she was prescribed diazepam.

I cried when Gemma took them because I hate what valium does to people and I love my wife very much. In the next month, Gemma was prescribed tramadol, then the next month she was given dihydrocodeine. I couldn't believe that the doctor was giving my wife all these medications that messed her up. Gemma was wrecked and I ended up back on the drugs, so I phoned my mum and told her that she needed to take our baby. It wasn't an environment that I wanted my son to be in, so my parents took him.

Gemma was a really good mum. She just lost her way and she became totally lost. Her brother was selling cheap valium and he came to her house and we couldn't get rid of him. He was hand feeding Gemma this fake diazepam and he helped to destroy her. He even had the cheek to tell people that his sister would lose our baby because she was on drugs.

Within a few weeks she was taken back to prison. She hadn't committed any crime. She was recalled for her own safety. All the tablets made my wife's life spiral out of control.

When she was back inside, Gemma found out that she was suffering post-natal depression and then she got diagnosed with borderline personality disorder (*BPD*), which is the same condition that I have.

BPD is also known as emotionally unstable personality and people who suffer this mental condition are prone to taking alcohol and drugs and prone to post traumatic stress disorder, which we both have as well. I have it because I was bashed about the head in an attack which nearly killed me.

So, after exactly eight months of freedom, Gemma was back in Cornton Vale. Then after a few months she was moved to Polmont. When I was in Polmont it was a Young Offender's Institution, but in later years, they opened a hall for female adults within the Polmont grounds.

Gemma told me that she liked Polmont and back in 2003 I loved it. Before I got married and became a dad, Polmont was the best days of my life. Then years later my wife was in there too, but I can assure you, it wasn't the best days of her life.

After 14 months back inside, Gemma went back before the parole board again, but was refused release. She was denied parole for another 12 months. She had to go back to Cornton Vale and work her way back out again. When she went back up for possible parole, she was given a further refusal for another nine months.

Over the years, I got to know Gemma through visiting her in jail and then so did my son. Nathan was a baby when Gemma was taken back to prison and he got to know his mother inside jail visits. Social workers got involved and I knew that if I didn't stop drinking and taking drugs then I would lose access to my son. Nathan is my whole world, so I had no option but to get clean and sober, but I couldn't stop taking drink and drugs. I was trapped in addiction.

If I drink, I will crave drugs, so I prayed from the bottom of my heart for God to set me free from all my addictions. The Bible says *he who the son sets free is free indeed.* I knew my Higher Power was Jesus, so for my own son, I decided to follow the Godhead three in one (*father sprit son*).

My only option was to cry out to God to save me from losing my infant child. I love my son so much. Thankfully, God gave me a touch and delivered me from the devil's clutch.

Last Chapter & Final Thought

And where did it all start? With a cigarette at 10, then I tried smoking hash and drinking alcohol at 12. Then in the end up I got addicted to it all. With me it's all or nothing. I can't take anything, or I will end up back in my addictions. Even a cigarette will lead me back to other drugs. If I put a cigarette in my mouth, I will smoke it and then my life falls apart. I will end up back at rock bottom. I will take as much different drugs as I can get, so I won't even smoke. I will have a much better chance to stay sober and clean. For me I need to be in total abstinence.

I put a nicotine patch on to help me stop smoking. I even had two patches on at the one time, but then they both became itchy, so I took them off instead of scratching them that night. I then prayed to God to stop the cravings for cigarettes. The next day, I went a walk in Kilmacolm where I found two cigarettes lying on the ground. I picked them up and put them in my pocket. I never had a lighter on me, so I couldn't smoke any of them, but as I walked home with the cigarettes on me, I decided to throw them away. I also made a decision to surrender nicotine to God.

It says in the Bible *take one step towards God and he will take two steps towards you*, so I threw the two cigarettes away. Soon after this I was in my flat in Bridge of Weir in my bedroom. When I decided to get down on my knees to pray for God to help me with my temptations and just at that moment (*while I was on my knees*), I found a small bit of hash on the carpet beside me. I picked it up and I thought about smoking it, but then I decided to throw it out my kitchen window.

Life's all about choices and if you choose to take drugs, but then you want to stop (*and can't*), then God can save you. I've been brought up as a Christian and I prayed every day, but I didn't get there overnight. It's a journey that I'm on.

Although now that I'm straight, I've never been so happy in all my life. As I am now sober with my son and wife. Life begins at 30. That's when I got Gemma pregnant and at 31, I became a dad. God blessed us with our son.

God has set me free from drug addiction loads of different times, but I didn't take Christianity seriously. God was up in Heaven and I was down here. I lived a double life as a Christian and a drug addict. I chose to give in to temptation and I used again. I had to surrender my whole life and become a full time Christian. Christianity is a new lifestyle which isn't easy, but God is faithful.

God has delivered me from alcohol, but I could never take another drink because it would start the obsession again, where I would need another miracle. Even though I trust that God would deliver me again, I don't want to live in that misery for at least one minute. Instead I walk in my deliverance daily.

At the AA they talk about God as you understand Him and I understand that Jesus is the Son of God. I don't just believe; I actually know for a fact that God is real. My prayers have been answered and God has taken away my cravings for drugs and I am now free from addiction. I couldn't have done it on my own. Through the devil's temptation I got myself into this mess and it was my Saviour who got me out.

After being an addict for years, I don't want drugs anymore. My heart and soul have been changed by something supernatural. God has taken away the desire for me to take drugs. I was a tortured soul and now I have been rescued from my lifestyle of misery.

Ever since I was 15, I needed drugs every day, but now I need God. To me that's what God stood for - getting off drugs (*GOD*).

I want to be the best dad that I can be for my own son and with God's help I will be. You have to want to be a Christian and you need to fight through your temptations, but with God's help it is possible.

Life is finally good. For the first time in many a year, I'm actually enjoying myself. I couldn't even remember what it was like to live a happy life. I merely existed and the life that I was living was a miserable existence. I didn't have a quality of life and now it feels great when I wake up in the morning to not be chasing drugs.

I used to wake up every morning desperate. Then when I was intoxicated, I would become desperate to get sober. Eventually I hated drugs. All these substances were controlling and almost destroyed my life.

I loved taking these substances, but then when I got addicted my life became a misery and I turned to God to set me free, which he did. Since I became a father, whenever I took drugs, I felt guilty. Now the Lord has made me happy and filled me with joy.

Although who knows what will happen next. Only God knows if I will stay sober or die alcoholically. Even though I've been set free, I could still make the wrong choices and end up dead in my addiction.

If I drink again the sugar in the Buckfast along with my diabetes would make me drop dead. Plus, I would batter my body with different drugs for weeks which could also cost me my life. Before I took drugs (*and when I was on them*) I ate a lot of sweets and chocolate along with drinking lots of juice.

The devil makes work for idol hands, so I know I need to keep busy or the boredom will kill me. I've only ever worked five days my whole life doing landscape gardening, but I got paid £1100 a month on benefits. The Bible says *the wages of sin is death* and I don't want to live the end of my life, dying at the bottom of a bottle.

The prophets also told me that I will be one who is addicted to God and I don't care what any unbelievers say. Being addicted to God is better than being on drugs, don't you care, to disagree.

Since I was 12 years old the longest I stayed off the drink for was 15 months (*twice*), but one of these times I was in jail. During my 30 months sentence obviously I went 15 months without any alcohol, but I drank the day I got out, without even realising I had a problem. However, when I realised I was alcoholic I managed to get sober for another 15 months a few years later but now I have beaten my record.

When I was a teenager I wanted to fight with different people and now that I'm older I have to fight with the devil. Temptation is a curse, but God promises to show me a way out.

I was killing myself with drink and drugs, but now that I'm sober, I don't want to die young. I want to watch my son grow up, but this can only happen if I remain sober and clean. I took drugs for all of my teenage years and in my twenties I drank alcoholically. All these substances robbed me of my adolescence.

Some people don't believe in God, but how can they deny when I have been delivered from my addictions? I thank God for the life I live now. My last drink was 17th April 2018 and the last time I took drugs was 17th July 2019, so the question is am I still alive or am I gone? God promises to *restore the years the locusts have eaten,* but if I don't make it, this book is my eulogy.

Drinking myself to death was the life I led and through God's grace, I'm not yet dead.

For years I believed a lie, that I would be on drink and drugs until I would die.

At the AA I learned to take it one day at a time and meanwhile, I decided to make this book rhyme.

I have a personality disorder and an addictive personality too. God bless me (*God bless this personality*).

I want to tell my son even if he gets the bug never to try an offered drug. Because I did and for years I lived like a mug.

I wasted so much of my life intoxicated and Nathan was the best thing that could have ever happened to me. I just hope he doesn't have ADHD.

For my sobriety and recovery God gets the glory. I hope you've enjoyed my story.

(the end)

If you're not laughing, you're crying. And if this book made you laugh and cry, then at least I've done something right.

Nathan would have wanted this photograph on the front cover of his book but for publication reasons this was not the best course of action. However, the photograph on the front has a story too. Just ask yourself who or what does he look like with the backpack?